Read all of the adventures in the Ari Ara Series!
The Way Between, The Lost Heir, and Desert Song

The W̶̶ ̶

Between flig̶ ̶ ̶ ̶ ̶ ̶ ̶ ̶s third path ̶ ̶ ̶ ̶ ̶d young shephe̶ ̶ ̶ ̶ ̶t master it . . . ̶ ̶ ̶ ̶oys everything she loves! She begins training as the apprentice of the great warrior Shulen, and enters a world of warriors and secrets, swords and magic, friendship and mystery.

The Lost Heir

Going beyond dragon-slayers and sword-swingers, *The Lost Heir* blends fantasy and adventure with social justice issues in an unstoppable story that will make you cheer! Mariana Capital is in an uproar. The splendor of the city dazzles Ari Ara until she makes a shocking discovery . . . the luxury of the nobles is built by the forced labor of the desert people.

Desert Song

Exiled to the desert, Ari Ara is thrust between the warriors trying to grab power . . . and the women rising up to stop them! Every step she takes propels her deeper into trouble: her trickster horse bolts, her friend is left for dead, and Ari Ara has to run away to save him. But time is running out - can she find him before it's too late?

Praise for the Ari Ara Series by Rivera Sun
The Way Between, The Lost Heir, and Desert Song

"This novel should be read aloud to everyone, by everyone, from childhood onward. Rivera Sun writes in a style as magical as Tolkien and as authentic as Twain."
- Tom Hastings, Director of PeaceVoice

"Rivera Sun has, once again, used her passion for nonviolence and her talent for putting thoughts into powerful words on a page to recreate life and show to us the possibilities that can be, if we dedicate ourselves to *The Way Between*."
-Robin Wildman, Fifth Grade Teacher, Nonviolent Schools Movement, and Nonviolence Trainer

"Ms. Sun has created a world filled with all the adventure and fun of mystics, martial arts, and magic contained in *The Hobbit*, *The Ring Trilogy*, and the *Harry Potter* series but with deeper messages. There are not enough superlatives to describe this series!" *- Brenda Duffy, Retired Teacher*

"During times when so many of us, especially the young, are still figuring out how to make this planet more just and livable, this book couldn't have come at a better time."
- Patrick Hiller, War Prevention Initiative

"A wonderful book! It's so rare to find exciting fiction for young people and adults that shows creative solutions to conflict."
- Heart Phoenix, River Phoenix Center for Peacebuilding

"Rivera Sun pulls off an impressive feat, creating an original and exciting story that deftly teaches ways to create a world that works for all. An outstanding contribution to the field of nonviolence!" *- Kit Miller, Executive Director, M.K. Gandhi Center for Nonviolence*

Wage peace!

The Adventures of Alaren

- Stories for Building a Culture of Peace and Nonviolence -

The Adventures of Alaren

Copyright © 2020 by Rivera Sun

Rising Sun Press Works
P.O. Box 1751, El Prado, NM 87529
www.riverasun.com

Library of Congress Control Number:
2019914971

ISBN (paperback) 978-1-948016-10-0
(hardback) 978-1-948016-20-9
(ebook) 978-1-948016-21-6
Sun, Rivera 1982-
The Adventures of Alaren

To the mythmakers, everywhere.
May we change the stories we tell.

Other Works by Rivera Sun

Novels, Books & Poetry

The Way Between

The Lost Heir

Desert Song

The Dandelion Insurrection

The Roots of Resistance

The Dandelion Insurrection Study Guide

Rise & Resist

Billionaire Buddha

Steam Drills, Treadmills, and Shooting Stars

Rebel Song

Skylandia: Farm Poetry From Maine

Freedom Stories: volume one

The Imagine-a-nation of Lala Child

RISING SUN PRESS WORKS

A Community Published Book Supported By:

Karen Lane
Bruce Nygren
Maja Bengtson
DeLores H. Cook
Sid Sibo
Cody Riechers
Jayanne Sindt
The Learning Council
Brian Cummings
Shelagh Bocoum
CV Harquail
Sofian & Shefer Family
Gerry Henkel
Barbara Gerten
Caitlin Waddick and Ursula, Anika, Rustum, and Asim Zia
Darien & Glenn Cratty
Johnny Mazzola
Marirose NightSong
Daniel Podgurski
Jeralita Costa
Elizabeth Cooper
Leslie A. Donovan
Dolly, Xyler, and Adam Vogal
Ken and Gail Kailing
Manny Hotchkiss and Mary Ryan-Hotchkiss
Rosa Zubizarreta
Kristi Branstetter
JoAnn Fuller
Joe and Bella Schenk
Annie Kelley, Multifaith Peaceweaver
Ka'imi Nicholson, Wayne Bow & Ari Bow
Andrew S. Oliver

David Spofford
Jaige, Adam and Aubrey
Deborah Cooper
Scott Springer, Class Teacher, The Bay School
Beverly Campbell
Leah Boyd
Beth Remmes

. . . and many more!

Thank you.

The Adventures of Alaren

- Stories for Building a Culture of Peace and Nonviolence -

by

Rivera Sun

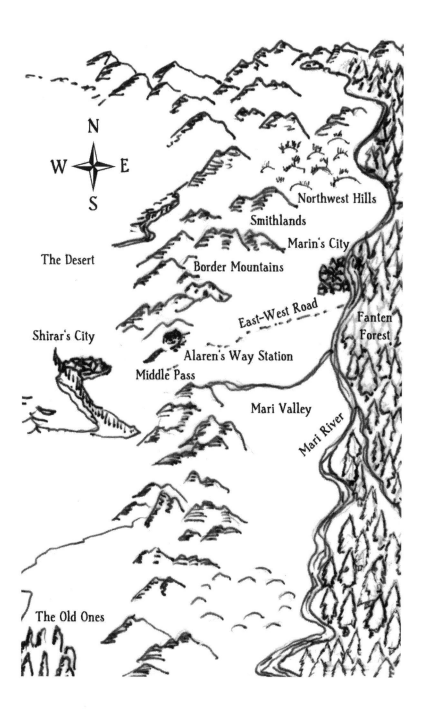

Table of Contents

Table of Contents, cont.

- Introduction -
by Rivera Sun

We are sitting at a turning point in human storytelling. The question is: will we pick up the pen that is mightier than the sword and tell a different story?

Every culture has its myths and stories. War cultures and cultures of violence use these myths to reinforce the use of violence and war. To create cultures of peace and nonviolence, on the other hand, we need legends and folktales that teach peace and valorize nonviolent heroes. Stories for a culture of peace would swap out sit-ins for swords, and reconciliations instead of revenge killings. Instead of the siege in the *Iliad*, the epic myths would be about blockades and picket lines. Instead of Robin Hood's archers, you might weave a tale of daring, merry activists pressuring rich people to divest, redistribute their wealth, and reinvest in economic justice. Instead of Wonder Woman using violence to stop wars and injustice, she might use protests, sit-ins, strikes, and demonstrations like Leymah Gbowee and the Women of Liberia Mass Action for Peace.

This isn't fairy tale thinking. There are plenty of contemporary references for a whole new style of legends and epic stories. Those alternative Merry Men might be modeled on Vinoba Bhave's Bhoodan Movement that redistributed land from wealthy Indians to landless peasants in the 1950s. These "sit-ins instead of swords" might be drawn from the lunch counter sit-ins of the Civil Rights Movements or the sit-ins at the peace talks that ended the Second Liberian Civil War. The field of peace and nonviolence has a vast wealth of epic and legendary tales to draw upon. These examples can become the basis of our fictional narratives and even a new mythology for humanity.

Courage, daring, cleverness, passion, mythic moments, tragedy and sacrifice, persistence and triumph: the stories of people like Leymah Gbowee, M.K. Gandhi, Dr. Martin Luther King, Jr.; Sophie Scholl, Wangari Maathai, Abdul Ghaffar Khan, Cesar Chavez, Dolores Huerta, Vaclav Havel, Andre Trocmé, and millions more have all the ingredients of classic myths. They offer us a marvelous opportunity to invent new stories beyond the mythologies of war and violence. The true stories also point to a kind of hero or shero, someone who is both ordinary and extraordinary, human and mythic at once. The real-life people involved in peace and nonviolence are as visionary as King Arthur when he makes his table round and as fallible as Arthur's troubles with Lancelot and Guinevere.

The Adventures of Alaren crafts a new kind of legendary hero out of the inspiration of real-life tales. I invented Alaren for the fictional world of my novel, *The Way Between*, but he refused to stay in that world. He may be fictional, but he makes himself at home in our real world. Alaren is a character that steps off the pages of fiction and winds up sitting next to us in spirit at our dinner tables. He pops into classrooms and conversations. He drops by in planning meetings for social justice efforts. He'll tap you on your shoulder during your next argument. He is a hero for our times, crafted from dozens of real-life inspirations. He is the Paul Bunyan of the peace movement, the Wonder Woman of nonviolence. Clever, creative, and courageous, Alaren offers us a kind of heroics we can all embody as we work for justice and wage peace.

This collection of short stories is designed to be used in the classroom, read aloud to young people, enjoyed by yourself, or retold to your friends and family. Each fictional folktale about Alaren is followed by the real-life story that inspired it. Discussion questions expand the two tales - fictional and real - into conversations on how to apply the ideas in your own life.

The Adventures of Alaren are stories for the growing culture of peace and nonviolence. At this point in human history, we don't need more stories of violent warriors and epic war battles. Thousands of years of human storytelling have been largely devoted to this purpose. Look where it has taken us. The mythology of war and violence is hurting us more than it is helping us. Now, it is time to transform our cultures and our stories.

The tools of nonviolence and the practices of peace are our contemporary superpowers. Nonviolent action is remarkably effective. Boycotts, strikes, blockades, protests, sit-ins, civil disobedience, etc., have been found to be twice as effective as violent means of waging struggle. Practices like truth and reconciliation, restorative justice, peacebuilding, and unarmed peacekeeping are revolutionizing the way we think about conflict. Our books, movies, stories, fantasy, adventure, and fiction need to catch up to the awe-inspiring, under-reported reality that is happening around the world. If we do not update our myths, legends, and folktales, we will be caught in the tragic cycle of violence for centuries to come.

The Adventures of Alaren - and, indeed, all of my novels - are my contribution to the movement to build a culture of peace and nonviolence. These stories inspire the imagination, spark our creativity, and dazzle us with tangible possibilities. They offer a different kind of hero or shero, one that is truly rooted in justice, armed with nonviolence, and powerfully waging peace.

I hope you will share these stories with friends and, together, lift them off the page and into your life.

Yours toward a culture of peace and nonviolence,
Rivera Sun

- A Word About Alaren -
From the Scholar Who Compiled These Tales

Alaren is a shadowy figure stalking the dawn of time. Few solid facts are known about him. The folktales and legends are full of contradictions and inventions. We do know that Alaren was the younger brother of the two founding kings, Marin and Shirar. He opposed their plan to split the world and refused to take a kingdom like his brothers, preferring to traverse the Border Mountains diffusing the ever-rising frictions between his brothers and their peoples. He married a Fanten woman, one of the forest-dwelling people who reside in shadows and secrets. They had at least one child, a daughter, though some accounts claim they had three.

It was she who introduced Alaren to the Way Between, a method of stopping fights and building peace. The Way Between began as a traditional dance of the Fanten people. Alaren adapted it into a martial art - or, as he liked to say, a non-martial art - one that could stop attacks without causing further harm. He expanded its principles into mass actions - protests and marches, boycotts and strikes - as he worked to halt war and wage peace.

Alaren lived to be an old man; there are numerous stories of white-haired Alaren's escapades. Some depictions show him hunched over his walking stick. He was a wanderer; legends say he crossed the Border Mountains a thousand times and that the Middle Pass was carved by his footsteps. It is also said that he stopped a hundred wars before they began. Once, it is rumored, the descendants of Alaren could recite these stories, but his lineage was persecuted many centuries ago. Those who were not tortured and executed were driven into hiding. Much knowledge was lost and Alaren's lineage died out . . . or so they say.

On Alaren's death day, when his spirit rose to join the great river of ancestors, it is said that the procession of mourners stretched across the mountains. Some stories say it was the feet of all who loved this rascally wanderer that carved the Middle Pass during his funeral procession. The people whose lives he had saved from death on war fields became a living river. Some legends claim that Alaren's spirit paused as it departed, seeing the people crying for his loss. At the edge of the ancestor river, he turned back and said:

"Wherever one speaks my name,
wherever my stories are told
wherever my tales are remembered,
my spirit shall live again."

With that, he abandoned the ancestor river to walk, as a spirit, over the mountains and among the people, sitting down at the hearthside, harvesting in the fields, spinning with the old women, tending sheep in the high pastures, trading spices in the desert.

For a time, many people claimed to have seen his spirit. Mothers would quiet bickering children by saying, "Stop your fighting. Alaren is here." In the taverns, the barkeep could break up brawls by hollering, "Greetings to you, Alaren!" as if the spirit had just walked in the door. The fighting pair would turn beet red in shame, dust off their clothes, shake hands, and end the fight in Alaren's name. There is also the historical record of King Marin's great-grandson, who called off a war because he claimed Alaren's ghost was haunting him for peace.

When war-weariness and grief set in, it was to Alaren's spirit that the people appealed. When his descendants and followers tried to stop wars, it was his spirit that gave them strength and inspiration. The truth of these tales is hard to trace. At the time, it was common for members of his Peace Force to lend credibility to new endeavors by claiming that Alaren had come to them in a dream.

In these times it is hard to imagine, but for hundreds of years after his death, Alaren's Peace Force was larger than the combined armies of Kings Marin and Shirar. Unfortunately, the Great Persecution of the followers of the Way Between crushed that beacon of hope and peace. The dangers and horrors of those times still flicker in the old people's eyes as they recall foggy stories told to them in childhood.

The collections of Alaren's tales are not supposed to exist. It is through great risk that they have been obtained. Even the written records were mildewed and crumbling, hovering on the edge of vanishing. With every old person's death, another faint reference to the stories of Alaren disappears. Their tales are foggy memories of stories their grandparents told them, many inaccurate or exaggerated. Truth and fiction blur in the folktale versions of what might have once been history.

Yet, the stories persist. This is a miracle . . . and a testimony to the enduring appeal of Alaren's adventures for peace. His courage, creativity, love, and persistence strike resonant chords in listeners throughout the years.

One of the folk traditions about Alaren that repeats in many tales has to do with a magical invocation of his name. In the tales, when people gave up all hope of peace, the words, "Alaren forgive me", would come to their lips. At the phrase, a vision of Alaren - or perhaps his eternal spirit - would rise before them, striding down a winding path, appearing in the river mist, winking across a crowded market. So, perhaps there is truth to the legend that his spirit still walks the world. Perhaps you will hear his laugh as you read these stories. Perhaps his tales will inspire you to help peace return to our world again.

- The Beginning -

Alaren was a peacebuilder from the beginning. Even as a small child, Alaren sought to make peace. He spent his childhood breaking up countless fights between his two older brothers. Alaren grew up in a time when "the world was whole", before his brothers split the kingdom and started wars. Back then, the world seemed large. The edges of his father's kingdom stretched from the Fanten Forest on the east side of the Mari River to the vanishing horizon of the desert in the west. All that would change in Alaren's lifetime.

- Alaren's Tricks for Peace -
How can he get his older brothers to stop fighting?

Once, when the world seemed small and the wilderness large, a young boy named Alaren grew up on a river island across the water from the major city of the land. His father was a king - which made him a prince, but in those days, there wasn't much difference between princes and pig herders' sons. They were all grubby little boys poking sticks into ants' nests and climbing trees. Alaren did chores like the sons of warriors and learned to read like the children of scholars. He was expected to mind his manners and make his bed just like everyone else. In those times, the royal family wasn't particularly stuffy, but they did have to make decisions about politics and laws and economics. Alaren found these subjects utterly boring. He'd much rather be outside playing by the river or in the forest. His greatest ambition was to be an explorer and travel all the way to the distant sea. He even set off in a rowboat once, but the river sailors caught him before he got very far.

Besides the fact that he was expected to be just like his father when he grew up - a stern and scowling king - Alaren's only other unhappiness in life was the constant fighting of his two older brothers. Marin and Shirar couldn't make it through a single day without one of them lobbing a punch at the other.

7

Alaren adored both of them and they (mostly) loved their skinny little brother as he scrambled after them trying to keep up. Marin and Shirar were barely a year apart in age, but they were four years older than Alaren - a lifetime to small boys as they got into mischief. His brothers were always hauling him over fallen trees, up rocks, and out of rivers. Alaren wanted to be anywhere they were . . . except when they were fighting.

"Those two'll kill each other someday," their sword instructor muttered under his breath as he hauled them apart and confiscated their wooden practice blades.

"They'll be the death of each other, mark my words," their tutor screeched, breaking up their squabbles in the schoolroom.

"Do you *want* to murder your brother?" their father thundered at them in his study after they got in trouble for a fistfight.

Alaren tried to keep them alive for several reasons. First, he loved them. Second, when they weren't fighting, they made life more interesting. Third, if they killed each other, *he'd* have to be king after his father. And he certainly didn't want that!

When he was very small, he simply wailed and screamed at the top of his lungs whenever his brothers fought. When he grew old enough to stand up on his own, he'd jump between them and try to shove them apart. Once he could run, he'd dash off to get the nearest adult. For a time, his brothers mocked him for being a tattletale and bluntly refused to let him play with them.

Alaren was more determined than ever. He spent hours in his room, muttering to himself, acting out the scenes between his two older brothers, and coming up with solutions. His carved wooden warrior served as a stand-in for Shirar (due to his block-headedness) and his old, fuzzy bear served as Marin (because he could be so stuffy). As for himself, Alaren emptied his toy box trying to find just the right thing to represent him. He tried a ragdoll - because he sometimes felt just as weak-kneed and flip-floppy. He tried a tower of blocks - because he could relate to getting knocked over a lot. He tried a carved horse, a paper hawk kite, and a stuffed bunny. Racing, soaring, and hopping, he played out a dozen scenes with his toys, searching for some way to break up his brothers' fights.

"The problem," Alaren muttered under his breath, "is that everything works once or twice, but doesn't work all the time."

He needed dozens of ways to intervene. Alaren tested out everything he could think of. He drew inspiration from all of his toys. The fierce, carved warriors gave him the idea to make horrible grimaces until his brothers stopped bickering to ask him what on earth was the matter with him. The wind-up mouse inspired him to run his fingers up and down their ribs to tickle them silly. The foolish clown made him try to do backflips to distract them from their argument.

When his brothers finally let him play with them again, Alaren had dozens of ideas for breaking up fights. He was almost eager for his brothers' next squabble, just so he could try them out. He didn't have to wait long.

As soon as they ran into the woods to build a tree fort, Marin and Shirar started arguing over who would be the king of the fort. Just as Shirar called for a duel and Marin grabbed a stick, Alaren shouted:

"Bear! Bear! Bear!"

And they hollered and took off running. Alaren tried not to giggle. (He'd gotten this idea from his stuffed bear.) Back at their home, panting breathlessly in the dusty yard, his older brothers started squabbling about who should lead the expedition to drive the bear away. Just as they started throwing punches, Alaren snatched up a bucket of water and doused them both. The ensuing water fight stopped the argument. (He'd learned that trick from his pet fish's suggestion to knock them both in the water.)

For the rest of the day and long into the next week, Alaren put his ideas to work. He challenged them to see who could stand on his head the longest. He made them hold a footrace to decide who got to ride the new horse. He made them hold their breaths to see who would get to have the last cookie. Alaren never ran out of ideas. He spent his childhood dreaming up new ones . . . and he used them through the rest of his life as he broke up bigger and bigger fights, even stopping wars.

~ The End ~

Behind the Story - Real Life Inspiration
Seeds of Peace

Sometimes, we think that only famous people like Dr. King or M.K. Gandhi can build peace and use nonviolence. In truth, everyone can build peace and people use nonviolence every day. Peace is as normal as stopping your friends or siblings from fighting. Nonviolence is as ordinary as standing up to a bully or helping an old lady to cross the street.

And *yes,* peace and nonviolence are extraordinary, too. With their tools and practices, people have stopped wars and thrown out dictators. They've won rights and protected freedoms. They've defended the environment and advanced social justice. Many of Alaren's adventures are inspired by these real-life stories.

Peace isn't just the absence of war. It is the presence of skills, tools, and practices that remove the underlying causes of war and build a world that works for everyone. Likewise, nonviolence isn't just the absence of violence. It is a word that describes hundreds of practices and tools from strikes and boycotts to peacebuilding and restorative justice.

This tale about young Alaren was inspired by the way people use role playing exercises, workshop activities, and even puppets to learn skills for dealing with conflict. When we want to learn a new skill - whether it's dribbling a basketball or intervening in a fight - it's helpful to study and practice before you try it out in real life.

Playing with his toys gives Alaren a chance to experiment with how to stop his brothers from fighting. He can practice what he will say and do. He can make mistakes and learn from them. This is something all activists and people working for peace and justice do regularly. With workshops, trainings, meetings, and gatherings, they practice the skills they need for the work they're engaged in. They do this in a variety of ways. Nonviolent Communication founder Marshall Rosenberg used puppets to model how language could help us navigate conflict. Activists take trainings and use role plays to prepare for taking action. They take turns pretending to be their opponents, learning nonviolent ways to deal with any potential heckling or pushback that might occur during an action.

In this short story, Alaren tries out a number of different approaches. He tries getting an outside authority, an adult, to intervene. He tries distracting his brothers. He suggests solving their quarrel with a non-violent competition like a footrace (coin tosses can also be used). He uses a bucket of water to change focus from fighting over horses to horsing around in a water fight. These are just some of the many alternatives to violence that we can use to resolve fights.

Role plays, trainings, and workshop exercises give us a chance to experiment with unfamiliar or new approaches. They let us test our skills, make mistakes, get feedback, and try again. Later, we can try them out in real life.

Discussion Questions:

- How else could Alaren have stopped his brothers from physically fighting with each other?
- Have you ever used humor, distraction, or any of the methods Alaren used when you've been in a conflict?
- Do you think it's important for someone to know different methods for how to address conflict? Why or why not?

- Alaren and the Fanten Trees -
How Alaren met the Fanten Daughter.

Though it is hard to imagine now, amidst all the great legends and jaw-dropping stories of his remarkable life, Alaren was once a gangly youth with hands too large for his limbs and an unfortunate resemblance to a stork. He was absentminded and prone to daydreaming at the dinner table. Frankly, his parents doubted he'd amount to much of anything. He was a smart boy, of course, but an odd duck, nothing at all like his older brothers, Marin and Shirar, who could hunt and ride and cross swords with the best warriors. Alaren was, well, squeamish, if truth be told, clumsy except on the dance floor, and terribly shy, which put a damper on his willingness to dance.

The day arrived when even his mother couldn't pretend he was a little boy - after all, Alaren was a hand taller than either of his brothers. (*If he would stop slouching,* his mother grumbled, *he'd be taller than his father.*) He had reached the age when he had opinions of his own and sometimes even dared to speak them. Alaren was a prince - not the most promising, but still third in line for the throne - but the prospect of becoming king sent a shudder down his spine. He detested the long meetings and stacks of reports that his father dealt with each day. He'd much rather spend the afternoons daydreaming in the shadowy

13

sanctuary of the great trees that covered most of the large river island.

On the morning that would change his life forever, Alaren was staring off into space. More precisely, he was gazing out the windows of the dining room toward the towering trees of the Fanten Forest on the East Bank of the river. From here, he could see the ragged scar of a recent clear cut. Alaren frowned. His people were not supposed to log on that side of the river. According to the ancient treaty, they shouldn't be there at all. The royal family's rights extended only to the west side of the river. Unfortunately, Alaren's father and brothers thought the solution to having too many people and not enough grain was to clear more land on the East Bank.

"It's not right," Alaren stated suddenly, setting down his teacup with an emphatic *clink* of porcelain.

Marin and Shirar paused midsentence in their quarrel over who would lead the expedition to clear more farmland. His parents looked up in surprise.

"What's not?" his mother answered. Her brow furrowed, anticipating unpleasantness. Her youngest child had a disconcerting habit of making outrageous statements as casually as asking her to pass the cream.

"The Fanten don't like it when you cut down their trees," Alaren replied.

Across the river, in the depths and shadows of the giant trees, lived a thin and long-legged people called the Fanten. Hardly anyone had ever seen them. It bothered Alaren's father that no one knew how many of them lived in the woods. It perturbed Marin that the Fanten had refused his attempts to buy their land. It enraged Shirar that they would not stand and fight in a proper war to see who, by force of arms, should control the East Bank.

14

It saddened Alaren that he knew so little about the Fanten.

He had seen them twice in recent months - a remarkable occurrence since they rarely interacted with outsiders. Alaren had met them when they came, silent and nearly invisible, to the grove of old trees on the river island to pay their respects to the thirteen trees they considered ancestors to the entire forest. Alaren often sat near the grove, sometimes reading, but mostly letting his mind settle like a still pond. The Fanten women had appeared, one after each full moon, bearing the same message, "Tell your father and brothers to stop killing our trees."

He had relayed their messages dutifully, but was only laughed at.

"Or else what?" Shirar mocked.

His family had ignored the second message as thoroughly as the first, but Alaren felt he had to plead on behalf of the Fanten once more.

"We shouldn't cut down their trees," he insisted to his family over breakfast. "They don't like it."

"No, of course not, dear," his mother answered with a sigh, "but one can't have everything in life. They have so many trees and we don't have enough farmland."

"It's just a few more acres," his father pointed out testily.

"And they're hardly putting up a fight," Shirar added. "If they really cared, they'd send out an army or something."

"Exactly," Marin put in, "they're just greedy."

Alaren stared at his family for a long moment, his face a mixture of disbelief and defiance. If they had noticed him, they would have seen the conflict raging in the quiet youth. Instead, the king went back to his reports, the queen busied herself with her breakfast, and his brothers resumed their quarrel. Alaren rose and left.

This all occurred in ancient times long before the

construction of the bridges. If you wanted to cross the river, you had to take a boat. Alaren had a bother of a time convincing a river boatman to ferry him to the East Bank. The dark-shaded woods weren't exactly forbidden, but no one was encouraged to go there. The Fanten had been known to trick a wanderer out of his life, soul, love, and fortune. But, Alaren's curiosity stood larger than his fear - a trait his mother claimed would be the death of him - and he wanted to warn the Fanten that the woodcutters were coming.

The ferryman departed as soon as Alaren's boots crunched onto the gravel of the riverbank. Alaren strode swiftly into the forest and was soon out of sight of anyone on the river island. He walked beneath the thick boughs with a thundering heart and a soft step. The trees towered like giants. Their trunks stood round as houses. Their canopies blackened out the sky. The tops rose so far above his head that he grew dizzy trying to see their height. Time stretched oddly in the forest. He soon lost track of how long he had been walking. An hour? A half day? All around, he sensed the forest watching him. His skin prickled. Just as Alaren paused to think about how to find the Fanten, the shadows slid apart and he was suddenly surrounded.

A band of Fanten women encircled him. They were young, not much older than Alaren, and wore the same spirited and defiant expression that he had thrown at his family when he left. Soft, grey-green dresses fell from shoulder to calf. Black woolen cloaks hung down their backs. Alaren didn't blink, afraid they would vanish into the gloom. The young women's dark skin matched the bark of the trees, a blushing cinnamon hue. They were thin, lithe, and eerily quiet. Steady, unblinking eyes pinned him into place.

"Who are you and why do you trespass in our woods?" one asked, coming forward as the others looked at her expectantly.

"My name is Alaren," he answered hesitantly. "I've come to warn you that my brothers, Marin and Shirar, intend to clear your woods this afternoon."

A set of trills rang out, angry and challenging. The Fanten's faces pinched in outrage.

"You must gather your men and fight them," Alaren urged.

An exclamation of disgust erupted from the group. The Fanten cringed with horror. The young woman who had spoken before tossed her dark hair scornfully.

"We abhor violence. It is an abomination."

"But how will you stop them, then?" Alaren cried.

"Watch and see, riverboy," she taunted, flicking a hand signal to the others.

Fluid as minnows darting in a stream, the band of women turned and ran swiftly through the forest toward the river.

Alaren wheeled in surprise and followed, feeling clumsy as an ox behind the fleet-footed Fanten girls.

"Where are the rest of your people?" he asked, struggling to keep up.

A shadow crossed the leader's expression.

"Hiding," she answered shortly. "As we have always done."

She didn't speak for a moment, but then took a long look at Alaren's earnest face and continued.

"Our elders urge secrecy and retreat, but the Great Mother Trees cannot hide and cannot run," she gestured to the forest towering over them. "Since time immemorial, the trees have protected us. Now, it is our turn to protect them from your brothers' saws and axes."

They broke out of the forest's edge. The line of defiant young women gathered near the river shore, blue beads glinting in the bright sun, black wool cloaks flung back over their shoulders. Without a word, they spread out, several women to a tree, and stood facing the river. On the far side of the swift, eastern channel, boats full of woodcutters were beginning to cross over. Alaren could see Marin and Shirar in the bows of the boats, pointing at the Fanten.

"What will you do?" he asked the young woman worriedly.

"We will block their axes. If they want our trees, they will have to kill us," she said with an eerie calm.

The boats landed. Marin and Shirar leapt to the shore, proclaiming their intent to cut the forest.

"No," the girl answered, throwing her arms around the trunk of the nearest tree. "You will not cut the tree! Not without cutting me down, too!"

The woodsman glanced at the princes, uncertain.

"Move," Marin ordered the woman.

"No," she refused, skin pressed tight against the bark.

"Cut her down," Shirar said coldly.

The woodsman swallowed nervously. He exchanged uneasy looks with the other woodcutters. One by one, each man shook his head. They were woodsmen, not warriors. They cut trees, not people. Shirar strode forward, took the axe, and lifted it. Alaren bolted toward the Fanten girl.

"No, brother!" he cried, flinging his body in front of the Fanten woman, arms spread wide.

"Out of the way, Alaren!" Shirar ordered.

"No," he answered, his voice cracking in fear. "I cannot let you do this."

"You side with a Fanten and a tree over your own brothers?" Marin chided him, striding forward.

"No," Alaren replied, shaking from limb-to-limb, knowing he was no match for even one brother, let alone both. "I do this for you, for your souls. I would not have the honor of our family stained with innocent blood. If Mother were standing here, she would beg you to lower that axe."

"She's not here, though," Shirar told him threateningly. "Move or I will cut you down with that Fanten girl."

"I won't move," Alaren replied. He tried to stop his hands from shaking, but couldn't.

"Move!" Shirar shouted.

"No!"

Shirar swung. Alaren gasped. Marin knocked the blow aside.

"Shirar!" Marin yelled, horrified.

A red flush climbed Shirar's face, but Alaren could not tell if it was shame or anger. He spoke quickly.

"Do not cut these trees, brothers," he begged. "We can dig irrigation ditches into the dry foothills in the northwest and open more farmland there. There are other ways besides this."

"Not easy ones," Marin grumbled.

"No," Alaren agreed, "but this option is no longer easy, not when these young women stand before you, ready to spill their blood before they let you cut these trees. Not when you would have to explain my murder to our mother."

He stared at his brothers until they looked away.

"I will find another way to feed our people," Alaren vowed.

Marin and Shirar exchanged frustrated looks, kicked the sandy bank, and spun on their heels.

"Back, back!" they ordered the woodsmen grumpily.

A trill of victory lifted among the young Fanten women, softly at first, then louder as the boats shoved off from the shore. Alaren felt strong arms hug his waist and then another hand pat his back. Suddenly, he was surrounded by the cheering Fanten, thanking him for his intervention.

"It's nothing," he said, ducking his head and blushing. "What if they come back?"

19

"Then we will be here to stop them," a deep, ancient voice answered.

Silence fell. Heads turned. A white-haired, wrinkled Fanten Grandmother stepped out of the edge of the forest with hundreds of Fanten on her heels. She scowled at the Fanten girl who had led the resistance.

"You were very naughty," she told the young woman, silencing her objections with a wave of her lined hand. "You were also right. We must stand to protect our trees. If we retreat forever, we will have nowhere left to go. Tonight, we celebrate. Tomorrow, we make sure our neighbors across the river know that we will guard our trees even if it costs us our lives."

"It won't," Alaren promised. "We will find another way."

The Fanten Grandmother turned her old eyes on him. They owed him a great debt.

"Stay and celebrate with us," she invited.

Alaren accepted. It was that night that he saw the Hundred Sacred Dances, that night when he first learned of the Way Between, that night when he watched the Fanten Daughter dance, and that very night when he lost his heart to her . . . but that is another story.

~ The End ~

Behind the Story - Real Life Inspiration
The Chipko Movement and the Treehuggers

This story was inspired by the real-life example of the Bishnois, the Chipko Movement, and the Treehuggers. In the west, the word "treehuggers" has been used as a slur against environmentalists, but the true story of the word goes back nearly two centuries to a tale of tragedy, courage, and victory. It began in 1730 with the Bishnois. A king in India wanted to cut down trees to build a palace, but the Bishnois objected. Protecting the forest was part of their faith. They stood between the loggers and the trees. The king's soldiers attacked. Three hundred and sixty-three Bishnois were killed in the bloody massacre. When the king heard the news, he was so ashamed that he stopped the slaughter of the others and protected the forest.

In 1973, two hundred and forty years later, deforestation was causing landslides, droughts, and economic challenges for the people of Reni Village in India. A movement erupted, called the Chipko Movement, in which people (largely women) invoked the Bishnois as they threw their arms around the trees to keep them from being cut down. This time, they were successful in their efforts to protect the forests.

Our real world is full of stories about people protecting trees. Wangari Maathai and the Green Belt Movement in Kenya work to reforest arid lands and stop desertification. Redwood Summer in California protected old growth trees with the help of a two and a half year tree-sit by Julia Butterfly Hill. A modern city gave their trees names and began to share photos and stories about them to rebuild people's connection to the trees. Stories like these circle the globe and give us all the courage to stand up to protect the forests.

Discussion Questions:

- What other stories have you heard about people protecting trees?
- What is courage? Does your definition of courage fit Alaren's actions, or do you think he was foolish to risk his life in this way?
- Discuss a time when you found the courage to do something that helped yourself or someone else.

- Alaren and the Way Between -
A gift from the Fanten.

All of his young life, Alaren had been searching for a word to describe the dozens of ways he stopped his brothers' fights. On the night of the Fanten's celebration after saving their forest, he finally found it: the Way Between.

Neither fight nor flight, but everything possible in between, the word came from a Fanten dance in which the dancer wove around and through all the others. Later, Alaren used it as his inspiration for the set of practices he used to stop wars and wage peace. Eventually, it would take on a thousand different forms and grow into a martial art. Or, as Alaren like to joke, a non-martial art - a physical way of blocking attacks and ending fights in a way that did not cause further violence. By the time Alaren died, the Way Between had inner and outer practices, individual and collective uses. Boycotts, strikes, sit-ins, blockades, marches, protests, peacebuilding, conflict resolution, restorative justice, and more would all become viewed as aspects of the Way Between.

But in the beginning, it was a Fanten dance.

To be precise, the Way Between was one of the Fanten's Hundred Sacred Dances. It embodied the thread of possibility that wove between all the elements of plants, animals, and minerals. On the night of the celebration, the young woman who had led the tree-saving effort danced the Way Between. Her name has been lost to time. We call her the Fanten Daughter, which is an honorific in her culture. Eventually, she became Alaren's wife. He came to the festivities as an honored guest as the Fanten men and women, children and elders all gathered to feast and drum and dance. Such a celebration we can only imagine. It is said that the dances that night whirled and spun with such joy that the height of the leaps and the speed of the backflips defied belief. The Hundred Sacred Dances were danced, in which the Fanten portrayed Rain and Shadow, Tree and Deer, Fire and Snow, and many more.

The dance of the Way Between explored the spaces between them all, the space where anything is possible. Neither this nor that, the Way Between's motions are what gave the Fanten Daughter the idea to neither fight with nor flee from the woodcutters. From this inventive dance, she was inspired to throw her arms around the tree and block the axe with her body, neither retreating nor attacking. This, she explained to the others, showed Alaren's brothers that the Great Trees were as alive as she, their sap was her blood; to cut them down was as heinous a crime as murdering her.

All this Alaren heard and witnessed as he gazed around him in wonder on the night of the celebration. The tall trunks of the trees towered overhead. Moonlight flooded the glen. The drums of the Fanten rang out, low and sonorous then sharp and rapping. The Fanten Daughter stole Alaren's heart with the first gesture of her dance. Throughout his life, Alaren could never say whether it was love for her that made him follow the Way Between, or the Way Between that wove their hearts together.

But this story is running ahead of its feet. Nothing

happened on the night of celebration; he watched in awe until sleep pulled the curtains of his eyelids shut. Alaren dreamt such wild dreams that he woke as sore and stiff as if he had danced until dawn.

A bright sun sent slivers of light down through the dark boughs of the trees. The Fanten had vanished, leaving him alone in the forest. He made his way back to the river, waved down a boatman, and returned to his family's home on the island in the middle of the Mari River.

There, he waded through mounds of trouble, his brothers' anger and his parents' irritation. He explained the importance of preserving the Fanten Forest. He suggested expanding the northwest farmlands through irrigation. He insisted that the farmers could plant the hearty grain *kerat* this year; it would feed the people and make clearing more farmland unnecessary. Obstinate resistance met his ideas, but he persevered. He was certain his solution would work. His father scowled over the logistics. His mother shook her head, wondering where her absentminded dreamer of a son had gone.

At last, Alaren snatched up the loaf of bread on the table.

"See this?" he demanded. "This is made with *pali* grain. It's popular because our royal family favors it, but it's hard to grow and takes twice the land for half the yield. If we switched to *kerat* bread, those same fields would produce enough to support our populace."

"I don't like *kerat* as much," his mother complained with a sour expression.

"So, you'd rather have people killed than eat your second-favorite bread?" Alaren asked, incredulous.

She shifted uncomfortably.

"Mother," he tried again, smiling winningly, "you are a fashion setter. When you drink elderberry tea, so does the nation. When you wear blue instead of red, so does everyone else. Now you have a chance to feed your people and keep peace with the Fanten. All you have to do is eat *kerat* bread."

She frowned in thought.

"I suppose," she assented, "when you put it that way."

Alaren nearly whooped in delight. He caught the yelp in time, and gracefully bowed to his mother, praising her wisdom and leadership.

And so it was. The queen ordered *kerat* bread to be served at her table. In less than a month, the nation's dining habits changed to follow her fashion. The rich merchants and minor lords put up a fuss, but Alaren convinced his mother to go visit them - and insist on being served her new favorite bread. The farmers planted fields of *kerat,* delighted at the prospect of a burgeoning market for a double-yielding grain. Alaren's father declared the East Bank and the Fanten Forest off limits, citing the ancient treaty. He commanded that an expedition take place to the Northwest Hills to explore the irrigation ditches concept. To Marin and Shirar's disappointment, he put Alaren in charge.

"And to think," his mother mused one morning, turning a roll of *kerat* bread over in her hands, "the solution to our problem was sitting right in front of our noses all this time!"

On the night before he was to depart to the Northwest Hills, the young Fanten Daughter came to him in a dream.

"Thank you," she said, "for saving our home. Ask a gift of the Fanten and your heart's desire shall be yours."

Alaren knew his heart's true desire - she was standing before him in his dreams - but he blushed with shyness and asked instead: "Might I learn the Way Between?"

The Fanten woman laughed like a bright peal of bells, suspecting his true desire in the blush that turned his skin the color of a rose.

"You may . . . and I will teach it to you," she promised.

Alaren's heart sank, remembering that he was supposed to leave soon for the Northwest Hills.

"It will have to wait," he told her sadly.

"Nonsense," she answered with a toss of her head. "I will get permission from the grandmothers to meet you in the northwest. Until then, I will dream the Way Between with you."

And so it was. For Fanten dreams are as real as day. Night after night, what she taught to Alaren in his sleep wove into his waking memory. Upon rising, the dance of the Way Between rumbled in his bones, leapt in his blood, and sang in his limbs. When the Fanten Daughter met him in the Northwest Hills, their dreams stepped out of sleep and into life as they danced the Way Between together.

~ The End ~

Behind the Story - Real Life Inspiration
Meeting Needs With Right Livelihood

In this story, Alaren takes the effort to save the Fanten Forest a step further by addressing the underlying causes of why his brothers sought to cut the trees down. Often times, a conflict cannot be resolved until the needs of both groups are met in another way . . . or, in the case of greed-based conflicts, the desires are released. By encouraging the planting of a different grain and building better irrigation in the northwest, he met the needs of his own people.

This story is based on many real-life examples of how to use constructive programs or alternative institutions to meet people's needs while working to stop an injustice. For example, the Just Transitions movement (part of the climate justice movement) seeks to join economic and climate justice by creating green jobs programs and re-skilling opportunities for fossil fuel industry workers. Homeboy Industries is an endeavor to merge social and economic services to help high-risk youth, former gang members, or recently incarcerated individuals connect to support services and employment opportunities. The Mondragon Cooperatives in the Basque Region of Spain broke through poverty, fear, isolation, and lack of opportunity after the Spanish Civil War using a set of industrial cooperatives. M.K. Gandhi, of course, had seventeen constructive programs that included everything from digging latrines to spinning cloth to making salt; all of these built Indian self-reliance and decreased economic dependency on the British.

These are also forms of what the Buddhists call *right livelihood.* In their spiritual context, the terms means earning your living without violating the rules of Buddhism, including not causing harm, being honest, staying focused and concentrated on spiritual understandings, being mindful, and more. But *right livelihood* has also expanded as a term that describes types of work and employment that do not cause harm to people or planet. These businesses and jobs don't exploit people, cause injustice, or profit from suffering. Since injustice is often the cause of conflict, including violence and war, it is important to create businesses that are fair and don't cause harm.

Like Alaren in this story, many people around the world are

starting to realize that if we want a peaceful world, our businesses have to be ethical, fair, sustainable, and nurturing to people and planet. Each and everyone of us has a chance to build peace by carefully choosing where we work and what businesses we support. Sometimes, this decision is very difficult. Other times, it's not hard at all. We should do what we can, wherever and whenever we can; and keep working on the harder parts until they become possible.

Discussion Questions:

- In this story, the conflict between the two groups arises over a dispute about the forest land. Can you name some other examples where two groups have gotten into conflict over land and nonviolent action was used to resist?
- To solve the conflict, Alaren's people have to change the kind of bread they are eating. What changes can we make in our lives to help protect the earth?
- What are some examples of right livelihood? Are you or anyone you know involved in work like that?

- Digging Ditches, Waging Peace -
Alaren convinces a reluctant lord to work for the common good.

The Northwest Hills spread in an undulating sea. Grassy crests swelled against the overcast sky. Dry earth pooled in the rifts between hills, black with deposits of ancient glacial minerals. Goats dotted the region, lipping the stalks of wild grasses. In the distance, the mountains loomed, snow-dotted even at the height of summer.

The emptiness and desolation could daunt the most stalwart man. Alaren's shoulders slumped at the overwhelming challenge of transforming this region into productive farmland. His crew drew up beside him, however, chins lifted defiantly at the challenge. Alaren had handpicked the engineers and architects, farmers and stonemasons, cartographers and geologists who would create the system of irrigation ditches. Some were old and experienced. Others were young, bursting with enthusiasm and fresh ideas. To them, the project was an adventure, not a problem.

They quickly began to survey the terrain, updating and confirming the royal archives' reports. At night around the camp fire, a young woman with a background in designing irrigation systems sketched her suggestion in the dust.

"It might work," confirmed the engineer. She was an older, iron-haired woman, quick to point out flaws, but even faster at finding solutions.

By morning, the sleepless crew had a rough idea of a plan.

"We will need workers," the stonemason pointed out, "and lots of them."

"I'll go to Lord Irram and see if we can hire some of his people," Alaren promised.

But when he reached the stone fortress, the lord refused to support the plan. Bellowing with scornful laughter, he mocked the entire notion.

"Channeling rivers from the mountains? Might as well try to squeeze the sky into a box," he jested, elbowing Alaren in the ribs as he guffawed. "It's a fool's errand, m'boy. My people have always been hardscrabble goatherds . . . and they always will be. They trade hides and meat downriver for valley grains."

"But if you channel the water, they'll be able to grow their own food," Alaren pointed out.

Lord Irram wouldn't listen - nor would he send workers. Alaren returned to his crew's camp dejected. To his surprise, he found that they had company. Over a dozen herders had gathered, sharing a meal and conversation, full of curiosity about the project.

"Bah," a herder spat when he heard Lord Irram's reaction, "he didn't ask us, now did he? There's plenty of herders who wouldn't mind a garden to call our own."

When Alaren asked if they'd like to work with him, however, they fell silent and shifted uneasily.

"Lord Irram wouldn't like that," one muttered.

"He might send his guards to rough us up," another admitted nervously.

"Or steal our goats," a third worried.

"Why would he do that?" Alaren asked, confused. It wasn't like they were stealing the lord's lands. The Northwest Hills belonged to the goatherds, not the lord.

"He wants us to stay poor," the first goatherd explained. "He takes twenty percent off all our trades. He owns the shipping barges and the marketplace."

The other herders noisily agreed. The lord collected his fees when they shipped hides south and when they bought the grain he brought in from the farmers downriver.

"That is a problem," Alaren sighed. He thought for a long while. Finally he spoke, "We can work around it . . . but I'll need one day of work from as many herders as you can gather."

"Just one day?" they asked, pointing to all the ditches outlined on the engineer's map of the Northwest Hills.

"Yes. Just one day to dig the most important channel of all," Alaren replied with a smile. "Can you do it?"

The goatherds exchanged glances. Lord Irram wouldn't bother them over a single day's work.

"Yes," they answered. "We can give you one day."

Later, after the goatherds had dispersed to round up other people, his team pulled him aside.

"Alaren, we can't dig the main ditch in a day!" they protested.

"That's not the channel I'm talking about," he answered. "Trust me. You'll see."

He broke them into six work teams. On the appointed day, hundreds of herders gathered. The planners passed out copies of the ditch system design. Like tree roots, it started thick at the taproot by the river in the mountains. It split into five smaller branches through the valleys between the hills. Each branch broke into two arms on the north and south sides of the slopes. From there, fingers of waterways opened at the tops of fields. A series of dams and sluices would control where the water would stop and flow.

The herders nodded in excitement. It was like building their own river system! They were eager to start digging, but to their surprise, Alaren didn't hand out shovels. He gave everyone a paintbrush and a bucket of white limestone wash. He pointed to piles of stones and told them to start painting them white.

"Today," he announced, "we'll put a trail of white-painted stones across the land and show where our ditches will be dug."

As the lines of white stone markers stretched from mountain to foothill to lowland rises, the design of the waterways became visible to all. The vision of the irrigation ditches lifted off the map and into reality. Soon, the goat herders called back and forth across the hills:

"I'll plant this field with potatoes!"

"This sunny field will be good for tomatoes!"

"I will put green beans here!"

As the goat herders ended for supper and stood around proudly admiring the outline of the ditches, Lord Irram rode up on horseback. Alaren walked over to greet him and noticed the man's eyes tracing the lines of white stones, imagining the flowing water moving through the ditches. He could see what Alaren had tried to describe to him before . . . and he could see the changes it would bring the region.

Before he could criticize, Alaren pointed to the sloping pastures behind Irram's stone buildings.

"Those are perfect fields for warm-season crops, south-facing and well-drained. If you had water there, you could grow tomatoes or peppers - there's a particular variety that my mother has been longing for. No one grows it currently, but she would pay dearly to taste it again."

Alaren saw the gleam of interest alight in the older lord's eyes.

"How long will all this take?" Lord Irram asked, gesturing

to the miles of ditches waiting to be dug.

Alaren sighed dramatically.

"Without steady labor . . . people to dig . . . it will take years," Alaren said, shaking his head regretfully, "and if the king loses faith in the project, he might seize the funds for other purposes. We might never get the water to your fields at that rate."

Alaren could see the lord thinking as the man scowled. Discretely, he gestured for the engineer and her team to come closer. They had practiced the words she raised in protest to Alaren.

"But you *must* convince your father, the king, to continue!" she exclaimed. "It opens up prosperity for this region - with self-sufficient farms, goats in the higher hills, specialty crops - you do the math, the yields are double the current system. Begging your lordship's pardon, you've done well with the challenges, but the profits on the goat and grain trades are nothing compared to the downriver market opportunities for irrigated field crops."

Alaren raised an eyebrow at her breathless monologue. She snapped her mouth shut, afraid she was overdoing it, but by her last words, the lord had promised to get the region's herders to work for Alaren's team. He took the engineer by the elbow and sat her down for a long chat about water mechanics. Before long, the expert farmer had been called over to consult about the best crops for selling downriver. As Alaren worked out labor contracts with the herders, his team carefully crafted a plan for Lord Irram that ensured he didn't force his herders to farm for his profit, but rather built self-sufficiency as the foundation for the region's wellbeing.

The next morning, Lord Irram himself wielded the shovel that broke ground on the main ditch. The engineer shifted close to Alaren and murmured,

"Is this the channel you spoke of?"

Alaren shook his head with a grin.

"No. The first channels that we opened were in the hearts and minds of the herders and Lord Irram. After letting the water of possibility flow through those places, the rest of the work is easy."

Those were the most important channels of all.

~ The End ~

Behind the Story - Real Life Inspiration
The Italian Gandhi: Danilo Dolci

This tale is inspired by the "reverse strike" of the Italian Gandhi, Danilo Dolci. A reverse strike is a day of work by hundreds or thousands of people on behalf of a much-needed project. In the 1950s, Danilo Dolci set out to transform the grinding poverty of Sicily, Italy. This put him in direct opposition with the mafia, a dangerous proposition. It was said that only his immense popularity among the people kept him alive.

Dolci knew that the mafia would not take the time or spend the money to do improvements in the slums. So, he organized hundreds of people to take a day to do volunteer work in their neighborhoods - a reverse strike. Over time, the reverse strikes also built solidarity, organization, and strength among the people.

Alaren uses a reverse strike to make the vision of the future visible using white stones. Why didn't he just dig the first part of the ditch? Because that would only have shown the people - and Lord Irram - how much hard work was needed. By making the vision of the project visible, he lit the spark of inspiration in people's minds.

Vision is a powerful tool when we're working for change - far more powerful, in fact, than just protesting against the problem. One useful framework to think about is to oppose the problem and propose a solution. Efforts that work on an "oppose and propose" platform have a greater likelihood of success.

Discussion Questions:

- Where else have you seen "oppose and propose" being used?
- Is there a problem in your community that would benefit from a reverse strike? How would you go about organizing one?

- The Day Marin and Shirar Split the World -
A Victory. A Swindle. A Tragedy.

Every story changes on the lips of the storyteller. Every tale shifts in the ears of the listener. Truth must pass through the veil of the eyes . . . and each person's sight distorts the image. The day Marin and Shirar split the world is told as a victory, a swindle, or a tragedy by each of the three brothers. Each version, if you were standing in their boots, is true.

The story of how the two princes broke one nation into two begins with the deaths of the king and queen. The plague that struck the river valley brought sorrow to every door. The whole world plunged into mourning. When the grief lifted, the nation found itself with a problem: the king had not named his successor. He should have named Marin, who was the first-born after all, but for years, he had avoided the arguments of his sons by refusing to choose one or the other. Some cynically thought it was the king's way of keeping Marin alive - if he had named Marin, then Shirar might have killed him to get the throne.

But now, they were really in a pickle. Without a clear successor, all three brothers were left in charge. As you might imagine, Marin and Shirar were constantly quarreling while Alaren tried to get them to compromise. Marin would flip tables in anger over Shirar's outrageous demands. Shirar would tear Marin's proposals into shreds. Both lunged for each other's throats at the slightest snide comment or sneering remark. Most days, Alaren settled for getting them to simply behave civilly toward one another.

After several months, numerous fistfights, and uncountable shouting matches, Marin whipped out his sword and told Shirar it was time to end this nonsense. Shirar drew his blade and swore they would fight to the death. The winner would take the throne.

Alaren flung himself between them, begging them not to duel, but Shirar shouted, "I would rather die than put up with Marin any longer!"

"Brothers!" Alaren pleaded. "Can't you just go to opposite ends of the land and ignore each other?"

He was thinking longingly of the quiet of the Northwest Hills where he'd be if not for the necessity of sticking to his brothers like glue to keep them from murdering each other.

A gleam came into Marin's eye.

"That's it!" he growled, glaring at Shirar. "That's what you'll do. Get out of here."

"Me?!" Shirar objected. "Why don't you leave?"

"I'm not going anywhere," Marin stated.

"Neither am I," Shirar vowed.

And so on for another two hours interspersed with bouts of sword fighting.

"Look," Alaren panted, dodging his brothers' blades and scrambling for the map of the world lying on his father's old desk, "there's plenty of room for both of you. Why don't you take turns living here and over the western mountains?"

"No!" shouted both brothers, whirling and slashing as Alaren held up the map like a flimsy shield.

It split into three parts as the two swords ripped through it.

A tiny sliver of the Border Mountains fell to Alaren's feet. In his right hand were the desert lands, rich with expensive ores, fine horses, and rare spices. In his left hand were the fertile farmlands of the Mari Valley, filled with fruit orchards, grazing lands, and productive fields.

Marin and Shirar stared at Alaren. Crafty gleams came into the brothers' eyes. At the same time, they each lunged for a piece of the map.

"I will take the desert lands," Shirar proclaimed, already plotting his trade routes and tariffs.

"I will keep the Mari Valley lands," Marin stated, counting up his wealth in the crops.

Alaren bent down and picked up the sliver of the Border Mountains, left between the two sword slices.

"You can have that," Marin told him magnanimously.

"I don't want it," Alaren replied sadly. "I want our peoples and lands to be whole, undivided, living together in harmony. Nothing good will come of splitting the world."

His brothers would not listen to his warning. Shirar stormed out. Marin smirked. Alaren wept.

As the day turned to night, the weeks turned to months, and the years spun out from that moment, Marin and Shirar grew vain, greedy, and bitter. On the day they split the world, each had initially thought that they had won a victory over the other. Shirar had chortled, seeing that his desert lands stretched much further than Marin's lands. Marin, however, dammed up the branch of the river that flowed into the fertile valley of Shirar's kingdom and forced Shirar to pay dearly for that water. Each was certain that the other brother had swindled him. Each eyed the unclaimed Border Mountains. Each began to claim ownership. And that is how the long history of all the wars began.

As for Alaren, he felt neither cheated nor victorious. He felt sad and worried. He fashioned for himself an emblem that was the map of the world made whole and refused to legitimate his brothers' claims. The sky, the birds, the deer, the seeds, the rain, the clouds, and Alaren continued to see the world as whole.

"Join me in supporting the whole world," he urged everyone. "Do harm to none and be good to all."

And he spent his life inspiring others to do exactly that.

~ The End ~

Behind the Story - Real Life Inspiration
The Partition of India and Pakistan

This story is loosely based on the partition of India into the two nations of India and Pakistan in 1947 after Gandhi's Indian Self-Rule Movement successfully ended British colonial rule. Mohandas K. Gandhi opposed partition; Hindu-Muslim unity was a major part of his campaign. He predicted - accurately - that partition would lead to bloodshed and violence.

Between 10-12 million people were displaced by the partition. A massive refugee crisis arose. Widespread violence broke out. Reports vary widely, but it is estimated that between several hundred thousand to two million people died. The violence during partition led to tensions between India and Pakistan that continue to this day.

India and Pakistan were not the only nations carved out of the aftermath of World War II. East and West Germany were formed. The Middle East and parts of the African continent were rearranged. Israel was created, beginning a series of conflicts between displaced Palestinians and new settlements of Israelis. Indeed, many of these divisions - which often seemed nearly as arbitrary as Marin and Shirar's sword slices across the map - set the stage for later animosity and wars.

At first glance, this story does not appear to be one of triumph and victory. But, Alaren's rejection of the divisions is the seed of his life-long actions for peace. He refuses to pick sides, caring instead for the whole world. As many of our real-life voices for peace do again and again, he warns his brothers that their actions will have dire consequences. Those who work for peace think carefully about the ways division and hatred build . . . and the ways we can cultivate connection and genuine caring for one another. This is the basis of preventing or stopping wars.

Discussion Questions:

- How have borders and walls affected peace?
- Where have they led to or increased hatred, violence, and war?
- What are the effects of building a wall between two countries? Can you name some examples to support your response to this question?
- Can a wall be a metaphor for something else that separates people? What might that be?

- Preventing War -

Once Marin and Shirar split the nation into two countries, tensions rose quickly. Trading routes and tariffs, border checkpoints, seizures of land in the Border Mountains, skirmishes and attacks all inflamed the two brothers' hatred of one another. Alaren spent years of his life racing to stop his brothers from sending everyone into battle. He stalled, delayed, and prevented the outbreak of war for decades. He also married the Fanten Daughter, raised a family, built a Peace Force, and crisscrossed the mountains working for peace. Here are some of his stories from that time.

- Alaren and the Whole Tax -
Two taxes are two taxes too much!

After Marin and Shirar split the world, Alaren took to the road. Some say he went north. Others say he went south. In truth, he went everywhere, but mostly he traversed the peaks and valleys, passes and high meadows of the Border Mountains. He spoke to children and elders, mothers and fathers, friends and neighbors about the dangers of his brothers' decision to draw lines on maps and make two kingdoms out of one. As word spread that the two kings had divided the world, the people in the dry lands aligned with Shirar and the people in Mari Valley supported Marin. But in the mountains, the shepherds and craftsmen, tanners and weavers, potters and masons scratched their heads.

"Which side are we on?" they asked Alaren.

"Be on the side of the whole world," Alaren suggested, pointing his finger to his emblem, a symbol of peace and an undivided world. "Do harm to none, be good to all."

He had painted a circle in black ink on a white flag. One side of the circle held the lines of sand dunes, the other held ripples of water. Under this banner, Alaren traveled swiftly through the region, but messengers of his brothers soon peppered the mountains like the wooly sheep. Each one declared that the villagers and craftsmen owed allegiance to their king and had to pay taxes.

"It's all well and good to support the whole world," grumbled the people of the Border Mountains, "but these double taxes going to Marin and Shirar will starve us before long."

Alaren thought for a moment, wondering if the Way Between offered any solutions to this problem. They needed a strategy that was neither fighting nor fleeing. If the villagers paid Shirar, Marin would attack them. If they paid Marin, Shirar would object. They could refuse to pay either brother . . . but then both brothers would be mad. There had to be a way to deal with this that didn't involve getting attacked by one or both of the kings.

"Here's what we could do," he told the villagers. "Pay half to each brother and I will send them a message explaining why."

He sent messenger hawks winging east and west. Each brother received Alaren's letter on the same day.

Dear Brother,

Since the people of the Border Mountains are being pressed to pay double taxes, I have advised them to pay half to you and half to your brother. When you put the world back together and fix what you have broken, then you will enjoy the whole of your taxes again.

Yours, Alaren

And that seemed to do the trick . . . at least for the moment.

~ The End ~

Behind the Story - Real Life Inspiration
Tax Resistance

Alaren's story about the Whole Tax is inspired by numerous tales of tax resistance, especially war tax resistance. Did you know that the term "civil disobedience" was coined by the writer and activist Henry David Thoreau when he refused to pay his taxes in protest of the Mexican-American war?

Governments have often struggled with people's resistance to paying taxes, especially war taxes. It is thought that tax resistance contributed to the collapse of several empires, including the Egyptian, Roman, Spanish, and Aztec.

Today, war tax resisters in the United States, among other places, hold back the portion of their federal taxes that would otherwise go to funding the military. They often write letters to the Internal Revenue Service explaining their decisions. Sometimes, they put the money in a fund with other war tax resisters that covers lawyers and legal costs if the IRS tries to collect the taxes or arrest the resisters. Other times, they donate the money to groups working for peace as an alternative form of "defense".

Tax resistance has been used in many struggles throughout history. One of the earliest examples in recorded history happened in Egypt during the Pyramid Age; a carving shows peasants being arrested for non-payment of taxes. Gandhi's Salt Campaign is considered an example of tax resistance; the Indians broke the British's salt monopoly laws, made their own salt, and thus did not pay the British fees for salt. The Women's Suffrage Movement in the United States included a tax resistance strategy based on the founding principles of "no taxation without representation". The United States' independence struggle had several tax resistance strategies. They refused to obey the Stamp Act (a tax on permits, printings, and papers). They boycotted British goods, depriving the British crown of import tax revenue.

In Alaren's tale, he uses tax resistance to oppose the splitting of one nation into two. It is a clever way to push back against double taxes . . . and an important action for the wellbeing of the Border Mountains people.

Discussion Questions:

- Would you engage in tax resistance? Why or why not?
- If so, what would you do with the money that you were not spending on taxes? Would you donate it to a cause? Put it in a legal fund? Something else?

- Alaren Under House Arrest -

Which brother would have the dubious pleasure
of arresting Alaren?

As time went on, each king stationed guards at opposite
ends of the Middle Pass. Anyone wishing to travel to one
country or another had to pay a fee. Marin and Shirar made a
potful of money, but no one else appreciated the nonsense of
the border crossing fees. More and more people began to see
the folly of splitting the world into two countries.

Alaren had set up a quiet little rest spot in the middle of the
pass. Here, he could bend travelers' ears as they partook of his
soup, slaked their thirst on his cool spring water, and rested
their feet in his way station. By this time, Alaren had married
the Fanten Daughter and they had a bright-eyed young
daughter. When travelers asked which country she belonged to,
she answered:

"I belong to the Whole World. I'm to do harm to none, and
be good to all."

This brought a smile to the weary travelers and opened up
conversations on how they felt about the splitting of the world.
In this way, Alaren heard the news, gossip, and grumbles of
each side of the world . . . and each side of the world carried
stories of Alaren's kindness, soup, and strange ideas about
restoring the Whole World back home.

51

Perhaps Alaren's older brothers might have accepted the half payments of the Whole Tax - after all, it was a lot of bother trying to argue with Alaren, chase down the unpaid taxes, or try to take the payments from the tax collectors of the other brother - but then more and more people began to join Alaren in calling for the two countries to reunite.

"You see," Alaren argued, "just because a couple of powerful men decide to rip a map in half, it doesn't mean people wake up the next morning feeling any different. You're all still the same people who were once one people."

The falconers of the desert agreed.

"You can tell a horse he's a hawk all you want," they grumbled, "but that doesn't mean the horse will fly."

"Aye," sighed some of the merchants of Mari Valley, "if the old king and queen saw this, they'd be rolling in their graves."

When the tax collectors came knocking, more and more people began to send half their payments to one brother and half to the other, calling on them to repair the Whole World.

If Marin and Shirar agreed on only one thing in their entire lives, it was that they wouldn't share a kingdom ever again. This business with Alaren and the Whole World had to stop. Each king sent a troop of soldiers to arrest Alaren. As it happened, they arrived on the same day. Alaren was weeding his turnip patch when he heard Marin's soldiers call out.

"Alaren! You are under arrest."

He stood up and squinted, then wondered if he had risen too fast. He seemed to be having double visions of soldiers in the yard. One group wore Shirar's red uniforms. The other wore Marin's blue.

"You can't arrest Alaren!" Shirar's soldiers shouted at Marin's men. "We're under orders from Shirar to arrest him."

Alaren sighed and reluctantly left the quiet of his garden as the soldiers bickered with each other. By the time he reached the yard, swords had been drawn and insults to each other's mothers had been exchanged.

"Friends, friends," Alaren said soothingly before they could start hurling insults about grandmothers, "this is a simple misunderstanding that we can easily resolve."

The soldiers stared at him.

"Each of you will send one man back to my brothers and ask which king will get to arrest me. Meanwhile, the rest of you will stay here. Shirar's soldiers will make sure Marin's soldiers don't take me away. And Marin's soldiers can ensure that Shirar's don't haul me off."

This seemed reasonable enough. The soldiers sent a man back to their kings and Alaren returned to his turnip patch, certain he'd be able to bring in the harvest. It would take months for his brothers to quit arguing over who had the dubious pleasure of arresting him!

And that's how Alaren cleverly managed to avoid getting arrested by his brothers, allowing him to spend the summer working to restore the Whole World.

~ The End ~

Behind the Story - Real Life Inspiration
Getting Arrested and Resisting Arrest

The stories of political arrests, house arrests, escapes from imprisonment, and the avoidance of unjust or deadly arrest by political activists are innumerable. There is no "right" or "wrong" way to handle a situation of arrest and imprisonment. It is all highly specific to the situation. Gandhi believed in civil disobedience of unjust laws; intentionally breaking the law to make it unenforceable and accepting the consequence of imprisonment. During Nazi occupation, on the other hand, uncountable numbers of people hid and fled to escape imprisonment and death. Denmark hid 6,000 Jews right under the nose of the Nazi regime and then whisked them out of the country to Sweden. After White South African anti-apartheid activist Tim Jenkin was convicted of handing out pamphlets, he broke out of Pretoria prison in 1979 along with two others and continued working for the struggle.

When it comes to arrests and imprisonments, there are many ways and forms of resistance. In this story, Alaren uses his brothers' conflict to allow him time to continue his work for peace and reunification. He is, however, stuck under house arrest with soldiers surrounding him. He buys time with this strategy, which allows him to formulate other plans. This is his choice on how to handle his threatened arrest. As for what he did after his turnips were harvested . . . well, that's another story.

Discussion Questions:

- When is it okay to break a law? When is it not?
- Can you name other examples of people being arrested for a just cause?

- Alaren's Escape -
Dancing the Way Between the falling snow.

The leaves dropped from the trees. Ice rimmed the stream edges, and still, Marin and Shirar's soldiers roosted in the yard in front of Alaren's way station. Hoarfrost whitened their whiskers and made their horses' breath turn visible on the air, and still, the two kings could not agree on who would arrest Alaren. At last, the day came when Alaren's Fanten wife peered into the secrets of the sky and read the future in the blank slate of the low clouds.

"Tonight, my love," she murmured to Alaren. "If you wish to travel, tonight the sky will cloak you in darkness and hide your tracks under snow by morning."

"I've no wish to wander on my own," he replied softly, looking over at their daughter by the hearth.

"If you've no wish to stay at home alone, you'd best be ready to walk," the Fanten woman told him sternly, "for I'm done living under the thumb of your brothers."

Alaren lifted his eyebrows and noticed small hints lying around the way station: the laundry folded, the nooks and crannies dusted, the weaving cut from the loom and the wool packed away. A fresh-baked batch of hardy cakes - traveling food that kept well and filled the belly - sat cooling on the counter. Their boots stood by the door oiled against the damp.

Alaren could see his wife was prepared to leave.

"Two friends of mine are coming tomorrow to help care for the travellers this winter," she mentioned to Alaren as they heard the sounds of the soldiers in the yard.

"Oh, we've more than enough hands to handle that," Alaren replied to tease her, "what with my brothers' men here to split wood and haul water to the horses."

"They make as much work as they do," she answered back, "for they've bellies to feed, too."

"Well, love," Alaren told her, "perhaps they won't tarry much longer."

He drew her close and whispered.

"We'll leave tonight."

They left under the cover of darkness. When a Fanten decides to vanish, even her own mother can't find her. And Alaren had been training in the Way Between for years; when he decided to move between the eyes of soldiers, he was no more seen than a shadow at midnight. As for their daughter, well, she could disappear in plain sight, that one.

Under the cover of night, the family fled, heading north in the pitch dark. When the daughter tired, Alaren carried her. His Fanten wife led the way, for her mysterious, forest-dwelling people have eyes that see without light. They reached the hidden safe-hold - an old robber hideaway carved into a cave - just as dawn began to crack the edges of the night. The entry was a stone tipped up against the others, impossible to spot on the jumbled hillside if you didn't know it was there. Snow began to fall as they crawled inside, weary to the bone from walking all night. The Fanten woman paused at the entryway, frowning at the sky.

"They'll be onto our trail," she warned Alaren, "the snow has come too late."

"The snow will be thick by the time they near us," Alaren reasoned, "and we'll light no fire and stay quiet."

Then they rolled the stone door back in place, huddling together in the dark and the cold. For the first part of the day they slept, holding their girl between them to keep her warm. The wind howled outside. Snow crept through the cracks of the door. They grew stiff and cramped but dared not go out. The afternoon turned colder than the morning. By the time the winter sun touched the westward mountaintops, their teeth were chattering hard enough to give them away.

"We m-m-must have a fire," the Fanten mother said. "Our li-li-ttle one will f-f-freeze."

Alaren opened his mouth to answer then froze stiller than ice. They could hear the sound of men and horses. Alaren put the edge of his cloak between their daughter's clattering teeth. Her mother put her ear to the ground, listening to the hoof beats through the earth. The sun dropped over the shoulder of the mountains, plunging them into shadows cold as death.

"They've gone," she said finally, "onward to the next village."

"C-can we have a f-fire now?" the little girl begged.

Alaren and his wife exchanged worried looks. Slowly, in despair, they shook their heads. The smoke could be seen a long way off. The soldiers would be too close still. The Fanten woman took her daughter inside her cloak and tried to hold back tears. Dusk deepened toward night.

"Come, love," Alaren said finally, an idea flashing in his mind. "Let's dance."

"Dance?" she answered. "Have you lost your mind?"

"If we must die of cold, let us have one last dance together," he answered.

He rose and rolled back the stone.

"Come, darling," he said to his shivering daughter. "Dance with your father."

She was too cold to argue and let him carry her outside where the black night tried to bite the life out of them as the daylight faded. Snow flurries fell, light and spacious.

"Try this," he told the girl, "dance with the snowflakes. Find your Way Between them."

That caught her interest; she was a girl who loved a challenge. Alaren showed her - or tried to, for his limbs were clumsy with cold and stiffness. When a snowflake smacked him in the nose, she laughed.

"Not like that," she chided, giggling.

"Show me then," he said with a wink to his wife.

The Fanten woman had crawled to the door of the cave and was watching them with a tired smile. The girl began to move in the snow. The dance heated her blood. The chilled blue in her lips gave way. A rosy flush bloomed on her cheeks. Alaren held his hand out to his wife.

"Come, love," he invited again, "dance with me, for I suspect we won't die this night after all. If I'm to live a long time, I wish to spend all of it dancing with you."

All night long, Alaren's family danced the Way Between the Falling Snow. When the sun rose, they slept warm in the cave. When night fell again, they moved onward. For many weeks, Marin and Shirar's soldiers tried to find Alaren and his family, but they vanished into the snow, no more visible than the wind.

~ The End ~

Behind the Story - Real Life Inspiration
Dance Resistance

Dance has been used as a form of resistance in numerous struggles. Enslaved African-Americans used dance to teach and preserve their culture through song and motion. During the anti-apartheid struggle in South Africa, funerals and mourning dances were used as a form of protest when demonstrations were banned by the government. Dance was so vital to the independence movement of Trinidad and Tobago that dancer Beryl McBurnie was credited with getting people ready "to handle independence psychologically and healthily". One of my favorite protest tactics is the flash-mob, where people gather unexpectedly in a public space and dance as a protest. A good example of this is the round dances used by Idle No More in busy shopping malls during the holidays to raise awareness about Indigenous rights and First Nations struggles.

These are just some of the stories of how dance has sustained courage, preserved culture, and worked for justice.

Discussion Questions:

- Can you explain how dance can be considered a form of resistance?
- What other stories of dance being used as protest or resistance have you heard?

- The Stonemason's Choice -
Baclan the Builder can make palaces for kings
. . . or he can build peace for his people.

Alaren was about to get himself in a whole lot of trouble . . . again. He had finally, after months of hiding in the mountains, convinced his brothers not to arrest him. Unfortunately, he suspected that he was soon going to give them new reasons to lock him up. But, if it was a choice between doing what was right and doing what was easy, Alaren would always do what was right, even if it meant climbing mountains or finding needles in haystacks. He couldn't stomach an injustice even if it came wrapped in a five-layer cake with a cherry on top.

Ever since the fateful day that Marin and Shirar "split the world" and divided the land into their two countries, Alaren had scrambled to build a movement to restore the whole world. Two countries meant two armies and two armies inevitably meant war. Alaren worked hard to prevent violence from erupting between people who had once been neighbors, fellow citizens, and even family.

On this particular day, Alaren strode down the hot and dusty streets of Shirar's newly-claimed capital city. The desert town was a sweltering maze of stone walls and twisting alleys. He searched for the house of Baclan the Mason, the chief architect of Shirar's planned palace at the north end of the city.

61

He rounded the corner and ducked as a clay plate came hurtling out the door of a dwelling.

"I won't!" a cracked old voice hollered. "Your forbearers have lived in this house for four thousand years."

"Yes, mother, and it's as old as the ancestors," a man argued, dodging the metal platter that she tossed out the door with surprising force. He held out his hands to block the kettle that followed.

"I want to die in this house!" the old woman's voice called out.

"And you will . . . when the walls collapse on you!" he warned, cowering against the wall of the neighbors' house.

"Then fix it, you worthless son. What good is it to have a stonemason in the family if you won't repair your family's house!"

"Shirar has a new house for us."

A rude splutter of sound erupted, followed by a stream of teacups that smashed right at the man's feet.

"Not great-grandmother's cups!" he cried, trying to catch one of them.

"I'll smash every last piece of your ancestors' inheritance and burn the rugs," his mother threatened. "I'll rip up your father's song sash and hang myself in disgrace."

The burly man sighed and shook his head.

"You won't do that," the man muttered. "Your spirit wouldn't be allowed to come back and haunt me."

"I heard that!" the old woman shrieked, racing to the door. "And - oh, hello Alaren."

The mason whirled in surprise.

"What are you doing here?" he exclaimed.

"I asked him to come and talk some sense into you," his mother chided.

Alaren hid a smile. Balla, mother of Baclan, was an old friend of his. Her family had lived in this city for thousands of years. A month ago, she had sent him a messenger hawk with a perturbing message: Shirar was bribing people with honors and awards to persuade them to renounce Alaren's stance of maintaining peace. Her son, Baclan, had been offered a fortune to build Shirar's palace and the man had accepted.

That fiend is buying off our people like a scoundrel dangling pretty jewels in front of young girls' noses, Balla had written. *He offered to make me his advisor, can you imagine? I gave him a piece of my mind for free. Go apologize to Marin and fix the mess you've made, I told him. He'll get my advice whether he wants it or not. I won't support his nonsense just to live in cushy splendor in Shirar's prison of a palace.*

Upon seeing Alaren, Balla sheepishly stopped hurling the kitchenware at her son and invited the tall, lean man in for tea. She ordered Baclan to bring the kettle she'd just thrown at him, whispering to Alaren that she'd never have hit him. Her son lumbered in with a grumpy expression and cleared off a wooden chair, gesturing for their guest to sit. The house was in disarray, half-packed and half-scattered from his mother's furious refusal to move. She'd come within inches of ripping up their ancestors' prized song sashes that told of their great deeds. Alaren picked up a length of silk and studied the inked script.

"When they made a song sash about you," he asked Baclan, "what will it say? How will your name be remembered?"

The man sat down heavily in the chair next to him.

"If I work for King Shirar, I will be remembered as Baclan the Brilliant, builder of palaces," the man grumbled.

"Humph. You'll be remembered as Baclan the Boastful who turned his own mother out of her ancestral home," his mother scoffed. "Baclan the Traitor who built bloodthirsty Shirar's empire and started a thousand years of war with his brother. Baclan the Idiot who sold out his honor for a fancy apartment."

Alaren drummed his fingers on the table.

"Baclan, I'm surprised at your choice," he remarked quietly. "You were always a man of honor."

"It is an honor to build Shirar's palace."

"On the way here," Alaren said, "I saw children begging for food. How can you let Shirar spend a fortune on luxuries instead of feeding his people? How can you accept his money?"

"I can give it to those children," Baclan answered.

"But you cannot give as much as Shirar will take in taxes to build this palace . . . and then to maintain his army . . . and then to build forts and treasuries and so forth," Alaren pointed out.

Baclan was silent at that.

Alaren met and held his eyes.

"You know why I am here."

The mason nodded. All of his mother's friends were talking about how Alaren was asking people to refuse appointments in Marin and Shirar's governments. Many of his friends had refused the honors, awards, and titles the two rulers were handing out like candy to children. Alaren had persuaded them to play no part in dividing the world. He asked them to refuse to give honor or legitimacy to Marin and Shirar by accepting their money and titles.

"I cannot tell you what to do," Alaren said softly. "Your heart must tell you that. But I leave you with one question."

He held up the song sash of Baclan's ancestors.

"When your great-great-great-granddaughter sings the song written on your sash, what will it say?"

Alaren set the silk down, thanked Balla for the tea, and departed. He had many houses to visit that day.

In the end, Baclan turned down Shirar's offer and fixed his

64

mother's house instead. We know this from his great-great-great-granddaughter's descendants who still sing the song written on an ancient sash about Baclan the Big-Hearted who chose to care for children instead of kings; Baclan the Brave who dared to tell Shirar that it was wrong to build a palace when children were hungry; and Baclan the Builder who raised money from the rich to build houses for the poor. To this day, Baclan remains so famous among the desert-dwelling people that to make a "Mason's Choice" is to do what is right, not what is easy; to care for the vulnerable instead of the powerful, and to fix your mother's house instead of building palaces for kings.

~ The End ~

Behind the Story - Real Life Inspiration
Renouncing Honors, Awards, and Titles

A method of nonviolent action that has been used in many struggles is renouncing honors offered by one's opposition group. Rejecting their honors, awards, titles, and appointments can undermine their credibility or legitimacy. By refusing to accept such honors, people can protest a government or institution they feel is unjust. Gandhi urged the supporters of Indian Independence to give up titles and honors bestowed upon the Indian wealthy class by the British colonial government. He saw how such honors had been used historically to "buy off" the Indian upper class, and strengthen the position of the colonial government. When thousands of

Indians renounced these honors, the British found themselves having less sway and even less power over the Indians. Meanwhile, the credibility of the India Self-Rule Movement gained traction as powerful Indians stated publicly that they no longer supported the British.

The nonviolent struggle scholar Gene Sharp reports in *The Politics of Nonviolent Action: Part Two, The Methods of Nonviolent Action* that during the Indian nonviolent struggles, "Sikh soldiers in large numbers returned their war medals, and thousands of other Indians relinquished their titles. The famous poet Rabindranath Tagore surrendered his title of British knighthood."

A more recent example of this occurred when Iraq War veterans, following in the footsteps of Vietnam War veterans, tossed away their medals at a NATO Summit in Chicago in 2012. Other protests that took place in Washington, DC, included throwing medals over the White House fence in protest of on-going illegal and unjust wars. The concept of renouncing honors also applies to organizations and institutions. Corporations, in particular, use community grants and awards to ingratiate themselves into a community and build trust and loyalty. While this might be a reasonable action for an ethical and sustainable business, when it is used to suppress public outcry against an exploitative and destructive corporation, it may be time to renounce the honors and awards the corporation bestows.

Discussion Questions:

- What is the benefit of putting the good of all members of your community ahead of your own self interest, as Baclan did?
- What was it that made Baclan reluctant to listen to his mother, and why did he listen to Alaren? What changed his mind?
- If you had to choose between tangible gains, like money or fancy houses, or intangible gains, like honor or reputation, how would you decide?

- Hagar's Oath -

Alaren asks an old friend to stand up for peace.

As his brothers gnawed like rats at the edges of the Border Mountains, trying to expand their territories, the call for war grew louder. Each king planned to invade and seize the unclaimed land that Alaren refused to take. Each threatened to "liberate" the mountain territories from the "threat" of the other brother. Alaren scrambled to stop both of them. Some of his efforts held the tenuous balance of peace only for a short season, but in Alaren's view, even one day of peace was worth the efforts of a lifetime. Hagar's Oath is one such story of how the Blacksmiths of Noor ensured peace for years until some of their fellow craftsmen betrayed them for greed.

The Blacksmiths of Noor lived in the northwest region of Mariana in a territory known as the Smithlands. Here, the hardscrabble hills hid iron ore in their bellies. The forges roared and the anvils rang. The smiths devoured mountains and shipped river barges of gleaming steel south down the Mari River, letting the current carry plows and pitchforks, saw blades and shovels. When talk of war flew in the screaming cries of messenger hawks, the barges began to carry swords, battle-axes, shields, and spears.

Yet, for all the legends that claimed the smiths were magical monsters of molten fire, Alaren knew they were as human as the next. Years ago, when he had dug and designed the irrigation ditches for the Northwest Hills, the smiths had asked him to design a similar system in their rocky hills. He even brought them a rare, hardy grain that thrived in stony fields. He had shown them how to survive on more than their forges.

So, when the barges brought the instruments of death and destruction to Mariana Capital, he knew the handiwork of his friends and traveled upriver to plead the case of peace.

The Noor clan was tall and rugged; even the women were burly as bears with biceps built from swinging sledgehammers and bending steel. All who worked the forges had singed eyebrows and blistered fingers tempered against the heat of their work. Alaren's old friend Hagar lifted his feet off the floor in a great bone-cracking hug and told him he looked more like a stork than ever. They shared stories over mugs of ale that made their chest hairs bristle. Alaren greeted Hagar's wife, three boys, and admired his darling infant of a girl.

"What brings you north, king's son?" Hagar asked him.

"I'm trying to stop my brothers' war," Alaren answered honestly.

Hagar looked askance and grumbled that he'd heard Shirar deserved a sound beating for the way he was nipping at the Border Mountains like a mongrel stealing scraps from a feast.

"That's not precisely what's going on," Alaren replied, rubbing his temples and explaining that the feud and skirmishes had been instigated by both brothers. He had hoped, he told the big smith, that he could persuade him to stop making such fine swords for Marin - the king didn't need encouragement in his plan to kill hundreds of people over his squabble with Shirar.

"Hagar, my friend," Alaren explained, pointing to the smith's sons as they wrestled over some bit of disagreement, "would you give your boys swords to slaughter each other over who gets to keep a toy?"

The smith bellowed to the lads to quit their yammering and shook his head at Alaren's question.

"Those two?" he replied. "Never. Why, they'd skewer each other without thinking and regret it all their days."

"So it is with Marin and Shirar," Alaren remarked, shaking his head over his two older brothers' quarrelsome, warring ways, "and this spat they're having over who gets to keep the mountains is nothing more than a boys' fight."

"It's a war, Alaren," the smith scolded, as if the size of armies made a difference.

"Would you dole out your blades to your boys' friends and let them charge at each other in the common room?" Alaren retorted.

"Ancestors, no. Their mothers would fry me over my own forge. They'd screech that I'd as good as murdered the lads myself!"

"And so it is with nations, Hagar," the stork-like younger brother of the kings said wearily. "They might not screech, but the ghosts of the dead will. Your blades will be cutting open rivers of blood across the land."

"What do you want of me, Alaren?" Hagar asked helplessly. "If I don't make the weapons, someone else will."

Alaren confessed that he'd come north not just to obtain Hagar's promise to stop forging weapons. The Blacksmiths Guild Council met in a fortnight. He wanted the Blacksmiths of Noor - the most respected in all the land - to speak for peace and to try to get the council to make a solemn pledge to refuse to make weapons for kings who fought like children over toys.

"The warriors will make their own weapons; clumsy things, nothing more than blunt hunks of metal," Hagar grumbled.

"Where will they get the steel and iron if not from you?" Alaren pressed.

"From the farmers' plows, no doubt," Hagar complained.

"Let them turn their plowshares into swords," Alaren commented bitterly, "so at least their hunger will stop their fighting."

Hagar stroked his bushy beard and stared at his sons. Wars, once started, were hard to halt. Every death cried out for revenge, and those killings for more vengeance, in a vicious cycle that quickly swallowed whole generations. If he started a war now, would his grandsons still be fighting it?

Hagar looked at his darling little girl. The women in his family were tougher than the men. If he made swords for war, would one of those blades wind up killing her in battle someday?

"I'll do it," Hagar vowed, "I'll give you my oath not to forge weapons of war nor sell the iron to others. And I'll take it up at the council meeting."

And so it was that the Blacksmiths of Noor, led by Hagar of Noor, appealed to the council and convinced their mighty craftsmen to forge peace not war; to refuse to be pawns of devastation; and to be leaders rather than lackeys.

For many years, Hagar's Oath kept war at bay. It wasn't until Shirar's crafty warriors started up their own forges and broke with the guild council that war broke out. Then, when Shirar's army attacked, the Blacksmiths of Noor felt they could not refuse the plea for weapons to protect their own people against the onslaught. But Hagar of Noor never broke his oath. Throughout his life, he taught his trade secrets only to those who kept peace and forged plows. That is why today, we swear "by Hagar's Plow" to show that we keep our promises, whereas those who "break oath" sow discord, strife, and war.

~ The End ~

Behind the Story - Real Life Inspiration
Swords Into Ploughshares

This story draws from the Biblical injunction of Isaiah to "beat your swords into ploughshares and study war no more". War is made possible by the support of many trades and industries. In many countries, especially the United States, the military-industrial complex is huge and powerful. It is hard to imagine people taking a conscientious stand against war and refusing to sell and trade to the military. But that's exactly what Google employees did in 2018.

Project Maven was a surveillance technology being designed by Google to give the United States military better ability to target and hunt people with drones. The employees, many of whom had made a conscious choice to work in the civilian sector rather than in the military, protested the program and organized walkouts and public statements against it. Because of their efforts, the project was dropped and several other defense industry contracts were put off.

Another example to look at is a campaign called *Divest the War Machine*. This coalition of peace organizations uses protests, boycotts, and other actions to get businesses, funds, investment companies, and individuals to withdraw their money from the war economy. Academic and religious institutions, retirement funds, and private investors are all pressured by the campaign to stop financing weapons-making, surveillance systems, military contracting, and more. *Divest the War Machine* encourages investors to divest and to then reinvest in the Peace Economy. The Peace Economy is a set of industries that build peace, work for justice, increase sustainability, and promote the wellbeing of people and planet.

Whether we are investors or not, we can all make choices

that lead to peace rather than war. We all have skills, abilities, and resources . . . and we have a responsibility to think carefully about where we place our time and energy. And, as Alaren said, "even one day of peace is worth the efforts of a lifetime." No matter how large or small your actions, do what you can to work for peace.

Discussion Questions:

- What does it take to wage war? What kinds of resources, businesses, industries, equipment, and people are needed? How could these resources and groups refuse to work for war?
- Would you consider working for the war industry? Why or why not?
- What about the Peace Economy? Would you consider working for those industries? Why or why not?
- In the story, they talk about how, if the smiths get iron from the plows, the fighting will stop when people get hungry. What are some other ways that wars contribute to food shortages?

- Alaren and the Peace Force -
*How old women and flirtatious girls
launched Alaren's Peace Army.*

Peace hung as fragile as a hen's egg poised on a table's edge over a hard stone floor. The slightest breeze, a small jostle, or a loud shout could send the delicate balance toppling and crashing to pieces. With Marin and Shirar rattling sabers at each other, everyone was on edge. As the threats of invasion rose, people were drawing lines in the sand and picking sides. The tension could break into fighting at the least provocation.

Just this afternoon, one of the village boys from the Border Mountains thought he had heard a shepherd from the next village insulting his mother and nearly stabbed the other lad. Alaren had intervened, telling the boy he heard wrong and hurrying both of them along. (The shepherd had actually insulted the boy's dog, but Alaren felt it wise not to repeat that comment.) The local youths were furious with one another over the rumors that this village claimed it would support Shirar while that village stated it would support Marin. From what Alaren could tell, none of the Border Mountain villages wanted to support a king who sought war, but all of them wanted someone's support and protection if war did break out.

It was enough to give anyone a headache. Alaren scuffed the dusty trail as he rubbed his brow. A scowl wrinkled his features.

The boys' spat had been close. Too close. The region was one misplaced rumor and a knife throw away from erupting into skirmishes that would be used to justify entire wars. He couldn't be everywhere at once.

"If only I had a twin in every village," he sighed.

A sudden thought struck him. Alaren jolted to a stop. A gleam lit up his eyes. A grin split the frown on his lips and lifted the scowl from his brow. He spun on the trail and hurried back to the village.

Before long, the Border Mountain villages were abuzz with the news: Alaren was building an army.

"But for peace," the shepherds and tinsmiths clarified. "They won't carry weapons and they'll stop wars instead of winning them."

Astonished laughter echoed off the peaks. People thought Alaren had cracked his skull falling down a trail. An unarmed army for peace? Who'd ever heard of such nonsense? The young lads called Alaren a fool. The men rolled their eyes and went back to work. But when Alaren called a gathering in one of the central villages, some people showed up: the grandmothers and the girls. The girls came expecting to watch the boys show off, and the grandmothers came to gossip about the silliness of the young ones. When they saw that no boys or men had come, they raised their eyebrows and giggled or chortled (depending on their age) at the empty village center.

Alaren scratched the back of his neck.

"Where's your army, Alaren?" one of the old grandmothers cackled.

"Well, besides me," he replied with a sheepish grin, "I guess there's not a man in the Border Mountains brave enough to try to stop a war with his bare hands."

"Or crazy enough!" she teased.

Her friend shot her a grimace.

"If he's crazy, what does that make me?" she griped. "Seems like I've got to stop a war every night in my kitchen, these days."

Alaren's ears pricked up. Arguments over which king to support had set fathers against uncles, sons against cousins, and turned over many a dinner table lately.

"And how do you manage that, old mother?" Alaren asked respectfully.

Her gap-toothed smile broadened.

"I threaten to stopper up the ale until winter if they don't simmer down," she chuckled, "or else I'll dump a cup of water over a hothead to cool him off!"

The women laughed with knowing looks.

"Oh yeah?" her friend countered. "Listen to this: my sons were at their cousins' throats last week. I got so caught up in scolding them that I set the hem of my skirt on fire. That shut them up. They were too busy hopping to put the fire out!"

"I should do that!" another old woman exclaimed. "Or at least shriek and pretend I'm on fire the next time the daggers come out."

"Hah, that's nothing compared to my house," an old grandmother declared, vying for attention. "I had to let the pigs loose to break up my sons' squabbling in the yard. They couldn't fight each other - they were too busy chasing pigs!"

The old women chortled and clapped appreciatively.

One of the young girls tossed her hair and eyed her friend.

"We stopped a war the other day, didn't we?" she commented archly with a sly smile.

"Oh, that merchant from the Mariana side of the mountains?" Her friend groaned as she remembered the incident. "He'd have murdered that desert blacksmith the way you were carrying on with him."

One of the old women asked the friend what she did to stop the jealous fight.

"Why, I kissed him, granny," the girl shot back pertly, "and he wasn't thinking of nothing else after that."

The grannies hooted and hollered. Alaren listened with a smile. It seemed the Peace Force members had shown up after all. In every village, there weren't just a few Alarens, there were dozens of women and girls, diffusing fights, dispelling tension, and disrupting the brawls that could spark into the flames of war.

And that was how Alaren's Peace Force began - with a bunch of women, old and young, laughing over the near misses and close calls they'd had over the years.

In every village, Alaren and his growing Peace Force found the ways people were already de-escalating fights. From those tales, he helped them develop skills and strategies that others could use. Stories turned into teachings. Lessons turned into trainings. Gatherings grew in numbers and focus. They acted out the tales. They improvised new ideas. They took turns pretending to be their sons, brothers, and fathers growling for a fight. They tried out their grannies' strategies. They experimented with the girls' ideas.

And wouldn't you know, it wasn't long before the young men came to watch the girls, the old men came to gossip, and Alaren roped them all into joining the Peace Force.

~ The End ~

Behind the Story - Real Life Inspiration
Badshah Khan and the Servants of God

In 1929, in what is now Pakistan, a man named Abdul Ghaffar Khan founded a movement called Khudai Khidmatgar (Servants of God). Khan was known by a number of honorifics, including Badshah, which meant "king of kings". He was also nicknamed "The Frontier Gandhi". The Muslim man was a close friend of Mohandas K. Gandhi. Badshah Khan was a major organizer with India's Independence struggle and a brilliant strategist. The Khudai Khidmatgar, Servants of God, was a peace army: nonviolence, disciplined, and courageous. With 80,000-100,000 members, it was the largest peace army in the history of the world. They faced some of the worst repression from the British colonial government, yet remained resolutely nonviolent. They were a people known for their violence, but both Mohandas K. Gandhi and Badshah Khan felt that the Servants of God could apply their bravery in other ways, namely into a powerful nonviolent movement.

In addition to this example, Gandhi and his successors formed another group called the Shanti Sena Network. This organization trained people throughout India to work as peace teams to de-escalate violent conflict. Other real-life counterparts are groups such as Nonviolent Peaceforce and Peace Brigades International. These examples served as inspiration for this fictional story about Alaren's Peace Force.

Discussion Questions:

- Can you think of a time when you used humor to diffuse a potentially harmful interaction? What was the result?
- Can you imagine a Peace Force in your school, neighborhood, or community? What would it do? How would you go about starting it?

- Code Peace and the Whisper Web -
How the people rapidly mobilized to stop war.

As Alaren's Peace Force grew, people came from all over to train in the skills the villagers had developed. Desert dwellers and river valley residents joined the people from the Border Mountains. They invited Alaren to conduct trainings in the foothills on either side of the mountain range. Soon, his network of Peace Force members spread throughout the world. Over time, it grew to include thousands of people. They put out the fires of conflicts, countered untrue rumors of attacks, held wrongdoers accountable when authorities failed to act, and resolved grievances that, if left unchecked, could fuel hatred and animosity. They set up a messenger system to relay news and information - and to mobilize the Peace Force into action when needed.

When Marin threatened to seize the Border Mountains by drawing a new border on his maps, Alaren knew he had to intervene. Shirar was already bellowing about invading the mountains just to remind Marin that he couldn't have them. The problem was, Alaren couldn't be in two countries at once.

"What you need is a whisper web," his Fanten wife told him.

"A what?"

"A whisper web - a network of messengers who can

81

mobilize people to take action at a moment's notice. This is how the Fanten alert each other to danger. Our web stretches from the snow-covered north to the marshes of the south."

She pointed to a spider's web trembling with dew and stirring in the morning light. A fly shook the web. The spider darted out of hiding and snatched it.

"In our case," she explained, "the whisper web told us when it was time to vanish into the woods until the danger had passed."

Alaren pondered the concept. He didn't need his people to hide; he needed them to take action. But as he thought it through, he came up with a plan.

It took time to train people and set it up, but soon, Alaren's Peace Force was prepared to drop everything and flood the streets of Marin and Shirar's cities to decry their attempts to seize the unclaimed land. In this way, an entire city could mobilize in minutes. News - especially with the aid of messenger hawks - spread across vast distances in days. Streets could be filled in seconds. Entire industries shut down in moments as their workers walked out to protest.

In the beginning, there was confusion about what should trigger an alert - they couldn't shut down the cities over every rumor that one of the kings was eyeing the mountains. They'd never get anything else done! So, Alaren set up a system of sentinels: Peace Force members who worked in his brothers' courts were put in charge of sending out the first alerts. They watched the kings like hawks. When blusters turned into real threats and the orders for action were about to be given, they triggered the whisper web to take to the streets. The signal they used was: *Code Peace.*

Code Peace, they whispered to the chambermaids.

Code Peace, the chambermaids told the stable hands.

Code Peace, the stable hands called to the fishwives and vegetable sellers.

Code Peace, they told the cooks and seamstresses.

Code Peace, they told the bakers and barge captains.

Code Peace, they whispered until, at last, thousands of people flooded the streets.

The flash protests stopped the world. Merchant shops closed. Dressmakers left customers standing full of pins. Blacksmiths doused hot iron in cold water. Cooks pulled the pots off the stove. Teachers walked out of the classrooms followed by their students. Delays bogged down the cities. The kings had to back off from war to get their people to go back to work.

The Peace Force made sure the blame for work stoppages fell squarely on the two kings. *Stop threatening wars and invasions,* they said, *and we will go back to work.*

Until then, the Code Peace alert remained in effect.

~ The End ~

Behind the Story - Real Life Inspiration
Code Pink: Women for Peace

This story is loosely inspired by Code Pink: Women for Peace. The group formed in 2002, following the attacks on 9/11 in 2001. At that time, the United States was using a system of security alerts based on colors (Code Red, Code Orange, etc.). Code Pink recognized how ridiculous this system was - it was largely designed to instill fear and provide a false sense that the government was responding to terrorist threats. The peace activists organized as Code Pink: Women for Peace and sent out Code Pink alerts to mobilize people to oppose the threat of war with Iraq and then Afghanistan. Now, the group organizes on a wide variety of issues revolving around peace, anti-war, and ending militarism.

In this story, a rapid-response network is created to mobilize walkouts from work whenever the kings threaten to start a war. Rapid-response networks like this have been used numerous times throughout history on countless campaigns. Groups working to stop fracking in Quebec made a "Shale 911" hotline that citizens could call if they spotted the gas industry trucks in their neighborhood. Once the call went out, the people would be ready to come block the roads. A similar campaign with the Keystone XL Pipeline organized people with a Pledge of Resistance and prepared them to respond if and when the pipeline permits were approved. The number of people willing to engage in civil disobedience also provided a deterrent effect to the industry, warning them that building the pipeline would be costly due to the mobilized resistance.

In another story, during the independence movement in Estonia, the Estonian prime minister got on the radio and called her people to come protect their independent congress when the Soviet troops tried to shut it down. The people came in mass numbers, nonviolently surrounded the building and the Soviets in the courtyard, and then let the troops march away, defeated, without anyone being hurt.

Rapid-response networks can be powerful tools for stopping injustice and thwarting destruction and danger. If every community had one, we'd be living in a vastly different world.

Discussion Questions:

- Imagine if your community had a whisper web or rapid-response network. Would you be part of it? What would it be used for? What would you be willing to do if you were called into action?
- Share another story you've heard about a strike or walkout. What was the issue? What was the effect it had?
- What would happen in your town or city if a work walkout were to occur? Imagine your schools, businesses, stores, etc. were shut down. Who would be affected and how?

- Singing For Peace -
King Marin allows the Peace Force to sing
. . . but only the songs he chooses.

Alaren's Peace Force came from all sides of the Border Mountains. In the Peace Force, people from the east and the west trained, worked, and lived side-by-side. Around the evening fires, the members who came from the dry desert lands would start to sing the songs of their culture. The people from the green river valley would offer their ballads in exchange. Soon, melodies from all places were lifted by the members of the Peace Force. The group began to hold song festivals everywhere it traveled, teaching new songs of peace and sharing anti-war ballads.

There was a well-known playhouse in Mariana, just across the river from Marin's royal house on the river island. It was notorious for its anti-war skits and humorous shows denouncing the threats of war. The director invited the Peace Force to come sing in the theater. Alaren blinked at the bold invitation to take his message of peace into the center of his warmongering brother Marin's nation.

The words and melodies of your songs are on everyone's lips, the theater director wrote in her letter. *Please come.*

No sooner had Alaren and his friends agreed to come than Marin banned them from performing. A ferocious back-and-forth of legal arguments, letters, popular petitions, and negotiations ensued. After much travail (and many street theater protests mocking King Marin), Alaren's Peace Force was allowed to perform.

The night of the song festival, the theater was packed to the rafters with excited audience members. Alaren and the Peace Force were waiting in the wings when an official from Marin's administration approached.

"King Marin welcomes you to the city, and graciously invites you to sing any songs you wish . . . except for these."

The official handed over a long scroll with more than a hundred songs listed upon it. Alaren scanned it anxiously; the entire repertoire of the Peace Force seemed to be on the list. He informed his friends. The clock ticked closer and closer to curtain rise as the dismayed Peace Force members debated how to respond. Should they obey and simply sing old folksongs? Should they defy Marin? Maybe they could tell stories instead of sing? Perhaps they should just cancel the concert and hold it outside the city later?

Alaren listened silently. The director of the theater begged them to do something - anything - before the audience got up and left. Alaren glanced down at the scroll in his hands, reread the instructions telling them they couldn't sing any of the listed songs, and thought back carefully over what the official had said. A smile rose on his lips.

"I have an idea," he told his colleagues.

A few moments later, the Peace Force stepped out of the wings. The restless audience fell silent. Alaren stepped forward, holding up the scroll.

"My brother Marin says the Peace Force cannot sing any of our usual songs tonight," he informed the crowd, chuckling, "but he didn't say anything about *you* singing them."

The Peace Force picked up their drums and guitars, pipes and tambourines. With a laugh and a wink, Alaren and the Peace Force began to play the melody of one of their most popular tunes. Suddenly, the surprised audience members caught on.

One by one, they started to sing the words of the song.

Incredulous laughter broke out. A mischievous joy tingled in the air. All night long, beginning at the top of the list of banned songs and going straight down to the bottom, the people of Mariana sang Alaren's peace songs.

When Marin heard the news, he hurled his teacup against the wall and cursed. By banning Alaren from singing, he'd just made his people do exactly what he didn't want: with their own voices, his people had lifted the songs of peace.

And, they knew all the words by heart!

~ The End ~

Behind the Story - Real Life Inspiration
Pete Seeger Defies Fascism in Spain

In the 1970s, well-known folksinger Pete Seeger was invited to give a concert in Barcelona, Spain. The fascist government of Francisco Franco was still in power, though declining. The pro-democracy movement organized a day of music with Seeger as the headliner. Just before he went on stage, government officials handed him a list of songs he wasn't allowed to sing. It was his set list. So, Pete Seeger took the list, strolled onstage and held it up.

"I've been told that I'm not allowed to sing these songs." He grinned at the crowd and said, "So I'll just play the chords; maybe you know the words. They didn't say anything about you singing them."

100,000 defiant freedom singers lifted up the words as Pete Seeger strummed his banjo, filling the concert stadium with words their government had not wanted them to hear . . . words they all knew and had sung in secret for years.

Do you know what words are written on Pete Seeger's banjo? *This Machine Surrounds Hate and Forces It To Surrender.* It's a nonviolent twist to Woody Guthrie's guitar that read: *This Machine Fights Fascism.*

Another wonderful story about song as an act of resistance is the Singing Revolution in Latvia, Lithuania, and Estonia in 1989. These three nations wanted independence from the Soviet Union. Mass demonstrations were not allowed, so the Estonians drew upon their tradition of folk singing to hold mass song festivals. In this way, they built unity and solidarity for national independence. They also used many other actions, including establishing independent governments. In a dramatic demonstration for freedom, they formed a 420-mile long human chain of two million people that stretched across all three countries. You can watch footage of the song festivals in the remarkable documentary, the Singing Revolution.

Discussion Questions:

- Where else has music been used as an act of creative resistance? Can you give some examples?
- In what ways may singing support resistance?

- The Siege of the House of Marin -
Marin's citizens blockade the king's house.

Over the years, King Marin grew angry with his younger brother Alaren's constant meddling (as he viewed it). He disliked the demonstrations for peace in the streets of his city. He abhorred the strikes against war that Alaren called for whenever he threatened to seize the Border Mountains. Most of all, King Marin hated hearing that his people wanted him to "repair the world" and rule side-by-side with his odious brother Shirar, the King of the Desert.

So, the next time Alaren and his followers were spotted demonstrating in the city across the river from his home, Marin had them all arrested for disturbing the peace. He locked them in jail and swore they'd never see daylight again.

Before the day was out, his aide came huffing and puffing into his reception hall with an urgent request for Marin to come quickly. He led the king to the docks and handed him a telescope. Along the opposite bank of the river, the relations and friends of Alaren's followers had gathered, shutting down the port and refusing to let the barges and ships dock and unload.

"They refuse to leave until you release Alaren and the others," the aide reported timidly.

Marin scowled at the crowd. These weren't Alaren's usual troublemakers. They were, by and large, his upstanding citizens. They were wives and husbands, serving lads and seamstresses, proprietors of shops and alehouses.

"Ignore them," he told the aide. "They'll leave at nightfall."

He was right. The crowd dispersed as the cold and dark arrived. But at dawn, they were back . . . and there were more of them.

"Ignore them," Marin repeated.

And this went on for several days, then for two weeks, then nearly a month. Shipments piled up on barges. Merchants pulled their hair out at the delays. Trade ground to a standstill. As the snow started to fall, Marin thought they'd give it up. But they didn't. They lit fires in metal barrels, sang songs, and roasted nuts.

"Ignore them," he told his aide.

The man gave the hot chestnuts a hungry glance and sighed.

Later that week, his head chef and master of stores came to him in a fit of concern. They needed fresh supplies and the protestors on the river docks were keeping the boats from making deliveries to Marin's island.

"You can't ignore them, sir," the cook said reluctantly, "not if you like your meals."

Marin cursed his brother. He paced down to the shore, gathered his soldiers, rowed across the river, and ordered the people to disperse.

"We'd be glad to, sir," a woman shouted back to him as he anchored just offshore, "just release Alaren and my husband and the rest."

Marin turned to one of his archers.

"Fire an arrow into the crowd to warn them off."

"But, sir - "

"But nothing," Marin ordered. "Do as I say."

The archer fired. The crowd scattered. Then the people reassembled.

"Again," Marin ordered.

So the archer fired once more. The people leapt aside. Then they returned. This went on all day. At dusk, Marin's stomach rumbled. A supply cart drove up the street. Marin recognized the merchant who supplied his kitchen. The people halted the cart, spoke with the driver, and bought his wares. As Marin seethed, the people began roasting the food in a large stew pot. Marin's mouth watered.

"Come and join us," one of the women called out, "just release your brother Alaren and my sister and all the rest, and we'd be glad to share supper with you."

Marin ground his teeth.

"Go get the mainland troops and drive them away," he ordered his aide.

"I would not advise that, sir!" the aide squeaked. He cowered as his king spun on him with a snarl of frustration.

"Why not?" Marin snapped, eyes flashing.

"B-because, sir, half of them are already out there with the people."

Marin squinted into the gathering dusk. The aide was right. He hadn't recognized them in their off-duty plainclothes, but there they were, warming their hands by the fire alongside fishwives and sharing stew with street urchins.

He shivered and gathered his fur coat tighter around his bones. The last thing he needed right now was a dead soldier - particularly one that was killed in a street scuffle fighting with soldiers following his orders. He needed his fighters loyal and supportive of him if he ever managed to start a war with Shirar.

Marin gritted his teeth. He griped and grumbled for a long, hungry hour, then finally made a decision.

"Release the prisoners," he ordered.

And that's how Marin's own people laid "siege" to their king to win freedom for their friends, family . . . and Alaren.

~ The End ~

Behind the Story - Real Life Inspiration
The Women of Rosenstrasse

In 1943, Nazi leader Joseph Goebbels rounded up the Jews who were married to non-Jewish German wives. He had delayed sending them to the concentration camps in an effort to maintain the loyalty of the German women. But, he refused to wait any longer; he had boasted that he would make Berlin *Judenfrei*, empty of Jews, by Hitler's birthday.

As soon as he rounded up the men, their wives organized a mass protest to demand the return of their husbands. It was a daring act - and a dangerous one. Just a few days earlier, young Sophie Scholl and other members of the White Rose resistance group had been beheaded in Munich for distributing leaflets denouncing the Nazis. Now hundreds of women gathered in open defiance of Goebbels' effort to exterminate their husbands.

For a full week, as many as a thousand women protested on Rosenstrasse night and day, defying orders to disperse, withstanding threats of being shot to death. The German Gestapo office sat within earshot; the women persisted despite the danger. On March 6, as thousands of other Jews were being sent to Auschwitz, the husbands of these Berlin women were released. Even the thirty-eight Jewish husbands who had already been sent to the camps were returned to Berlin. It is said that the Rosenstrasse protest also halted the plans to round up the intermarried Jews in France, a change that likely saved thousands of lives. The German government felt that the dissent and visible signs of resistance would be detrimental to morale at that time. Releasing the men was easier than risking more uprisings.

When ordinary people display extraordinary courage and determination, amazing things can happen - especially when the actions cut off a major supply line of resources to the power holder, as Alaren's friends did when they stopped the food deliveries from going into Marin's kitchen. Like the women of Berlin, Marin's citizens also leveraged their social privilege on behalf of the imprisoned followers of the Way Between. Actions by allies such as these can be game-changers in nonviolent struggles.

The other lesson of this story is the importance of persistence and numbers. In both real life and fiction, the people persisted in demonstrating day after day, despite the cold weather and the dangers. They came back with more people each day and showed that they were determined to succeed. As nonviolent struggle scholar Gene Sharp said, "You can't lose if you never give up."

Discussion Questions:

- If this happened to your family members, what would you do? Would you protest like the women of Berlin? What else might you do to get your family members released?
- Dr. King and Mohandas Gandhi believed that if one accepted suffering for a just cause without retaliating with violence, then justice will prevail. Think about the story and the real-life examples. Do you agree or disagree with Gandhi and King's belief? Why?

- Alaren and the Messenger Hawks -
If only Alaren could send the children's letters . . .

Alaren was worried. Despite the best efforts of the Peace Force, the threat of war was rising. Over the summer, skirmishes and minor clashes had flared up between the two armies. Fears and lies had erupted among the people. For months, Alaren had been crisscrossing the land, listening to people and dispelling rumors, but a man can only be in one place at one time, and the rumors ran faster than the wind. The Marianans shrieked that it was attack or be attacked so far as the Desert People were concerned. The Shirarans, as the Desert People were called in the early days, argued that they had to attack the Marianans for the same reason. Each side believed the other side wanted to pillage their lands, steal their goods, and murder their children.

Alaren knew the truth: everyone was afraid and no one needed to be. The Marianans didn't eat babies (as the Shirarans claimed). And the Shirarans didn't bury people alive (as the Marianans claimed). And everyone would rather stay home than tromp over the Border Mountains and fight.

Everyone, that is, except the two kings Marin and Shirar. The older brothers of Alaren each sent out their soldiers to spread fear and lies and rumors, stirring up hatreds and prejudices so their people would pick up arms and march off to fight.

Alaren buried his head in his hands, thinking hard. The villagers of the Border Mountains had begged him to help. The two armies would collide on top of their villages if the war started. It spelled disaster for the villagers no matter which side "won". Alaren's Peace Force members were hard at work, but Marin and Shirar kept arresting them. He had tried to write letters to the newspapers, but Marin and Shirar threatened to shut down any publisher that printed his words. He tried to hire town criers to tell the truth, but Shirar hanged two and Marin bribed the rest into silence. Peace Force members on both sides of the border had answered his request to write letters countering the rumors; school children had written notes asking for peace, but while the sacks of letters were allowed to leave the country, neither Marin nor Shirar's border guards would let Alaren or his followers pass into their countries with them.

He was stumped.

Alaren sighed and settled his red cap over his head to shade the bright sun out of his eyes as he walked. He climbed the mountain path lost in thought, headed toward a little cabin tucked beneath the high peaks of the mountain. He had come to visit his friend Narwan, a master hawk keeper, to see if he could borrow a bird or two to send yet another set of letters to his brothers.

He was just lifting the latch on the gate when he heard Narwan shout.

"Look out!"

Alaren ducked as a snowstorm of papers fell on him from the blue sky. Squinting, he saw a black hawk wheel off and return to the short imp of a man who was frantically jogging down the slope.

"Sorry! So sorry!" Narwan called out, racing to catch the papers before the wind snatched them. "I've been trying to train the dratted things to drop messages from the sky - red caps are the signal, see - since my fellow hawk keepers report that Marin and Shirar are stealing my hawks and locking them up for collaborating with the enemy. By that, they mean you, of course."

Alaren grinned at his friend's long-winded explanation and lent a hand in snatching up the papers.

"Still needs a bit of work," Narwan confessed sheepishly. "The hawks just drop the letters at any red hat they see, not the one I want."

Alaren whooped and threw his handful of paper into the air like confetti.

"That's it!"

He spun Narwan in a dizzying circle, laughing.

"They'll drop the letters wherever they see a red cap?" he asked the hawk trainer.

"Yes, any red cap," the man complained.

"It's a miracle!" Alaren cheered.

"It's a dratted nuisance," Narwan argued, mopping his sweaty brow with his sleeve. "I've got to train them all over again - dozens of birds - because red caps are coming back in style these days."

Alaren threw an arm over Narwan's shoulders.

"Don't retrain them yet, old friend. I've got a job for your birds first."

Alaren managed to smuggle messages to the Peace Force members and on the appointed day, all over the two countries, red caps popped up by the hundreds. In the big cities and small villages, craft halls and farms, a fad for red hats seemed to sweep the world. Just as Marin and Shirar's spies and soldiers started to wonder about it, the cry of hawks echoed across the sky.

A moment later, letters began falling like snow, fluttering down into the outstretched hands of shopkeepers and seamstresses, merchants and miners, potters and carpenters.

"Why, they're letters!" a Marianan tailor exclaimed. "From Shirar's people."

Across the border, a spice merchant caught a fluttering paper and turned to the pickle-maker in the next booth.

"The Marianan children are writing to us," she said, looking at her neighbor's note. "They want us to keep the war from starting."

To the east and to the west, the falling letters were read by amazed eyes. People swapped them and shared them, comparing notes and reading stories of their counterparts' lives.

Marin and Shirar were furious, but they couldn't stop the clever hawks. With the true stories being delivered, neither king was able to trick the common people into joining their armies or supporting their calls for war. The looming threat of war dwindled and stalled . . . at least for the moment.

Narwan never did teach his birds to deliver to the right person in a red cap, but Alaren put them to work over and over again dropping letters and true stories into the hands - and hearts - of the people.

~ The End ~

Behind the Story - Real Life Inspiration
Sophie Scholl and Samantha Smith

In 1942, a group of young Germans formed the White Rose, a clandestine resistance effort that decried Nazi militarism and the war. In a time of intense repression, the group printed pamphlets in secrecy and left thousands of them all over Munich. Secret couriers brought the leaflets to other cities. While distributing stacks of pamphlets through the university, twenty-three-year-old Sophie Scholl tossed a handful down from the second story balcony. (This is what inspired the hawks in Alaren's fictional folktale.) A janitor spotted her in the act and she was arrested. Sophie Scholl and six of her fellow White Rose members were tried for treason by the Nazi regime. They were executed in 1943.

Sophie's heart-wrenching last words were: "Such a fine, sunny day, and I have to go, but what does my death matter, if through us, thousands of people are awakened and stirred to action?"

In Alaren's fictional tale, the idea for the letters from school children and ordinary citizens is drawn from the efforts to de-escalate the Cold War. Groups of peace activists set up US-Russia pen-pal societies and encouraged the writing and sharing of personal letters to counter the fear-mongering propaganda of the time. One particularly notable letter was written in 1982 by Samantha Smith, age 10, to Soviet leader Yuri Andropov, seeking to understand why the relations between the Soviet Union and the United States were so tense. To the surprise of many, Andropov wrote back:

"No one in our country – neither workers, peasants, writers nor doctors, neither grown-ups nor children, nor members of the government – want either a big or 'little' war. We want peace. There is something that we are occupied with: growing wheat, building and inventing, writing books and flying into space. We want peace for ourselves and for all peoples of the planet. For our children and for you, Samantha."

He invited her to visit the Soviet Union. She accepted and a diplomatic exchange ensued that helped to de-escalate the tensions over nuclear warfare.

When fear, hate, and propaganda cause people to dehumanize other human beings, nonviolent actions like leaflet drops and letter campaigns can re-humanize the people involved in the conflict. Humans are literally hardwired for peace and nonviolence. We have millions of empathy neurons in our brains. Our empathy neurons are what make us feel sad when we see other people crying or feel pained when we see others in pain. It's an evolutionary tool that makes us want to stop fighting and start helping each other. But, it only works if we see or hear true stories about the human beings on the other side of our conflict.

If the propaganda machines have fooled us into thinking of our enemies as "demons" or "monsters" or any type of dehumanizing, derogatory slur, then we're less likely to seek a peaceful resolution to our conflicts. We become frightened and willing to do terrible things like perpetrate genocide, use nuclear weapons, commit war crimes, or engage in massacres. This is how the military circumvents our empathy neurons: they train soldiers to view the enemy as less than human. Efforts like Alaren's, Sophie Scholl's, and Samantha Smith's can play crucial roles in returning us to our senses, engaging our empathy, and kick-starting our courage and creativity toward finding peaceful resolutions.

Discussion Questions:

- In either the fictional or non-fiction examples, why do you think the letters made a difference?
- Have you ever written a letter to a child or person from another part of the world? If so, what did they write back? If not, what do you imagine they'd write you?
- Describe a time when you discovered something about someone that surprised you, and led you to think differently of that person.

- Mourning the Death of Peace -
Sorrow at the start of war.

Alaren shaded his eyes. A messenger hawk sped over him, a dark streak against the blue sky. A shiver ran up his spine. Premonition chilled him. To the west, black smoke heaved from a burnt village. Last week, an assassin tried to kill Marin. Under torture, the man confessed the location of his home village on the west side of the Border Mountains. In the dead of night, Marin's soldiers razed the village and executed every last soul. The message was clear: try to kill our king and we'll kill you.

Now, Shirar's messenger hawk shot like an arrow eastward. Alaren suspected that it bore a declaration of war. Shirar's army had recently moved into the neighboring village, telling the frightened people that they were now under the protection of Shirar.

Alaren sank to the ground as the hawk vanished over the stony pass. He buried his face in his hands, his heart heavy with despair. He had worked so long and so hard to prevent this day from coming. He had worn holes in his boots traveling between his brothers' lands. His small children had grown into lanky teenagers and then young adults as he halted his brothers' looming war, day after day, month after month, year after year.

Now, the war he had so long held at bay had arrived. Alaren

wept for his children. He wept for all the children. He wept for the whole world. While Marin and Shirar would undoubtedly hold mass celebrations and rallies promising a swift victory, Alaren could only mourn the death of peace.

Don't give up, he told himself. *You can't lose a war if you never give up working for peace.*

And with that thought, he lifted his head. War may be declared: so what? He had always worked for peace . . . and he would keep working for peace until the last breath in his body. Every moment of peace was a victory. Every day a war was postponed, delayed, or prevented was a victory. Every second shaved off the end of war was victory.

No one should cheer the start of war, he thought, *only its end.*

Suddenly, he knew what to do next.

In Marin and Shirar's cities, Alaren's Peace Force took to the streets. Garbed in black robes of mourning, they wept and wailed as others cheered. They cried for the death of peace. They moaned and sobbed over the looming tragedy of war. They cast a shadow over the military parades. Their wailing interrupted the pompous speeches of commanders and kings. They were dragged away by guards, but the sound of their cries echoed in people's hearts. A sense of ominous warning flooded into people that no amount of drumming and trumpeting could drown out. By wailing and protesting in black robes, Alaren's Peace Force denied the two kings their cheering crowds and visions of victories.

And so it was that Alaren sowed the seeds of the war's end even as it began.

~ The End ~

Behind the Story ~ Real Life Inspiration
Women In Black

This story of public mourning draws inspiration from Women In Black, an international anti-war movement with an estimated 10,000 activists around the world. Founded in 1988 in Jerusalem, it has spread to many other countries. Women in the network wear black clothes and protest in public spaces. They often mourn the deaths caused by war, call for peace, and decry war crimes and injustice.

We often think of protests as angry, but the full range of human emotions - pride, sorrow, hope, vision, defiance, humor, and more - can be used during demonstrations for social change. The PRIDE parades are public marches by LGBTQIA persons showing their pride in who they are. After a tragedy, candlelight vigils are often used to lift up prayer and mourning, along with a demand for change. An environmental protest called a "Procession of the Species" organizes people to dress up as animal and plant species threatened by human destruction and both celebrate the beauty of those species and decry the dangers they face.

The more we can tap into our full range of human emotion and creativity, the more options we have for memorable, effective, powerful, and transformational action.

Discussion Question:

- What are some other examples of creative action that use different emotions?
- Describe some ways that people plant the seeds of peace in our real world.
- Can you think of a conflict where creative action using a wider range of emotion would have changed the outcome?

- Surviving War -

The raids, skirmishes, and war propaganda sowed hate and fear in people's hearts. Despite Alaren's best efforts, there came a day when Marin attacked Shirar and Shirar attacked back, and war broke out between them. On top of striving to restore peace, Alaren provided aid and shelter to displaced Border Mountain villagers, protected civilians against army attacks, and set up hospitals for all in need. The war lasted ten years, a full decade of Alaren's life. It is said that he began the war as a dark-haired man and ended it as an old man streaked with gray.

- The Peace Villages -
Building peace one village at a time.

Thock. Thock. Thock. Alaren hammered a sign to a post at the village edge. A cluster of curious children nudged and jostled behind him, looking at the sign.

"What's it say?" one of the boys called out.

"It says: if you went to school, you'd be able to read this sign," Alaren answered with a sigh and a chuckle.

"It doesn't say that," another child scolded with a giggle. "That's too many words."

Alaren turned and eyed them. Not one of the children could read. Some could spot a word or two, but the outbreak of war had disrupted lessons, burned schools, and killed teachers. With Marin and Shirar's soldiers charging through the region, everyday life had been upended. One day, the villagers were invaded by Shirar's army. The next day, they were occupied by Marin's army. The third day, the villagers ran into the nearby forest as the two armies fought in their village streets. Parents didn't dare send their children to school - they never knew when they might have to flee. That's why the youngest crop of children had not learned to read.

But that was about to change.

Alaren pointed to the characters painted on the sign.

"This is the name of your village, Clear Springs. And this means peace," he said, pointing. "And this means - "

"Village!" one of the girls shouted, recognizing the word.

"So it does," Alaren answered. "Clear Springs Peace Village."

Something had to be done. Here in the Border Mountains, both armies harassed the villages. Marin and Shirar's armies had been burning villages to the ground, seizing villagers as hostages, and executing people of fighting age. After many late-night arguments and much debate, the people of Clear Springs had decided to declare themselves a Peace Village, a refuge in the horrors of war. They would provide a safe space for the region's families, children, and elders. No weapons were allowed in the village proper. The people had to remain nonviolent and stay out of the armies of Marin and Shirar. Furthermore, they couldn't work as spies or guides for either side. The Border Mountain villagers wanted peace. If kings wouldn't make it, they would - even if it was just a tiny patch of the world called Clear Springs Peace Village.

"Here," Alaren called to the children, squatting down on the dusty footpath and picking up a stick. "Each of you copy that sign in the dust three times."

Anything new was a game to the children. Before long the footpath was covered with squiggly, but understandable characters. Anyone entering the village would walk right by or on the words. The message couldn't be missed.

"Come on," Alaren invited the children. "I have to hang two other signs and you can practice your writing skills at the other end of the village."

Peace. Village. Clear Springs.

Not a bad start to learning, Alaren thought. If all children learned those words first, the world would be a vastly different place.

~ The End ~

Behind the Story - Real Life Inspiration
The Peace Community of San José de Apartadó, Colombia

This story draws inspiration from the real-life example of one of Colombia's Peace Communities. Caught in the crosshairs of military, paramilitary, and drug smuggling violence, the Peace Community of San José de Apartadó was formed in 1997 by five hundred displaced farmers from seventeen different villages. It consists of a territory of multiple villages situated in the center of some of the most intense violence during the Colombian War. The Peace Community resisted the violence with a policy of neutrality and a refusal to carry weapons. They upheld the right of people to refuse to participate in the armed conflict. Community members worked together to farm, educate children, and maintain the community's non-combatant status.

The factions of the armed conflict responded by murdering many of the peace community members, including massacring six young people in front of the whole community. The initiative continued despite terrifying repression. The numbers of community members grew. Every time the fighting factions forced them to leave, they reoccupied the area. Over twenty years of resistance, 326 of its members were murdered, and over 4,000 human rights violations, including torture, were committed against them. Through it all, the community members remained resolute.

Today, the Peace Community of San José de Apartadó cultivates crops for cash, export, and local self-sufficiency. This is important because, by farming their own food, they can avoid being part of the drug trafficking that causes so much violence. The Peace Community has also crafted an educational program based on love of the earth and founded the Farmers University

114

of Resistance, which trains people in nonviolent action. Groups like Peace Brigades International have provided unarmed protective accompaniment to the community members, ensuring that human rights violations and massacres are either thwarted or registered by the broader international community.

Discussion Questions:

- What are some reasons why people would choose to create peace villages, even if it is dangerous?
- How can people remain peaceful and neutral when wars and fighting break out?
- Have you ever been the neutral person when your friends or family started fighting? What was challenging about this?
- What does it take for people to put their lives on the line for what they believe in?

- The Brothers Wall -

Two feuding kings can't divide a peace village!

In the Stony Pass, along the East-West Road, the two kings Marin and Shirar were building a wall. Two walls, in fact, because the kings were brothers and mortal enemies, and neither would cooperate with the other on anything - even on building a wall in the exact same spot. The walls ran along a recently invented border, each king claiming his territory went all the way to his wall.

To make matters worse, stone for stone, back to back, the two walls rose like twin serpents smack through the middle of a peace village. The stonemasons - a burly and dusty lot - shook their heads over the foolish pride of kings and shared mortar and tools with the opposing king's craftspersons. By the time the wall was built, the Stonemasons Guild - the oldest international guild in the history of the two countries - was founded. But that's another story.

Alaren heard about the ridiculous double wall from one of his Peace Force members, a woman who lived in the village. She had hiked the narrow and winding footpaths through the Border Mountains to find him. Alaren's Fanten wife added broth to the soup and broke out a fresh loaf of bread to feed the weary traveler. Alaren poked fresh life into the fire to ward away the night's chill as it clung to the shivering woman.

"We wouldn't be upset if they'd built their silly walls a hundred paces on either side of the village," the village woman complained. "Then we'd at least have a nice perimeter to keep wolves and warriors out."

But no. The brothers had built their walls straight through the village, splitting it in half like an apple. Families were divided. The village well - the only water source - was on the opposite side of the wall from half of the homes. Each day, they had to haul water up one flight of wooden stairs, over a plank bridge between the two walls, and down a second set of stairs. When they complained, the officials told them to move to one side or the other. When the villagers refused - shaking their heads in disbelief at the nonsense - the officials plunked soldiers down on the walls to oversee the daily traipsing back and forth.

"They think we've turned into enemy spies," the woman grumbled, "and they interrogate us for going to visit our grannies."

The woman asked Alaren to help the beleaguered Peace Village.

"Write to your brothers and talk some sense into them," she pleaded.

Alaren agreed, though he doubted that Marin and Shirar would listen to him.

Sure as pigs roll in the mud, his brothers refused to move their walls one inch - unless it was into the other brother's territory. Alaren - who didn't believe there should be any sides to this great and beautiful world - sighed in exasperation. He bid farewell to his wife and journeyed over the mountains to the village.

He spoke to the villagers on one side of the wall. He spoke to their friends and families on the other. At dawn on the third day of his visit, Alaren picked up a stone that was sitting on the edge of the east side of the Brothers Wall and climbed up the steps to the guard post at the top.

"Where do you think you're going?" Marin's guard challenged him.

"Invading in the name of Marin," Alaren said flippantly, tossing the rock up and down in his hand.

"You can't do that!" Shirar's guard objected, drawing close to the other soldier. "I won't let you through."

"I'm not coming through," Alaren promised.

The village woman walked up the steps on the west side of the wall, a stone in hand. She handed it to Alaren. He gave her his rock in exchange. They walked back down the stairs, crossed the village and set their stones down on the opposite sides of the village - right where the woman had said a set of walls would at least keep out the wolves. They each picked up another rock, returned to the double walls, and climbed the steps once again.

"Now what are you doing?" Shirar's guard demanded.

"Peacefully invading in the name of Shirar," the village woman answered as Alaren nodded.

"I don't understand!" the guards exclaimed at the same time.

Alaren winked.

"Friends, how would you like to report a great victory of expansion to your kings, won without bloodshed and without losing a single warrior? In fact, you don't even have to lift a finger."

Confusion creased their features.

"We're putting these foolish walls where they should have been built in the first place - if they had to have been built at all," Alaren told them.

"But that's Marin's land on that side!" protested Marin's soldiers.

"It'll be the same amount of land once we're done . . . just the walls will be in a different place," Alaren pointed out. "We're just moving some stones, that's all."

"But, but, it's not up to us," the guards spluttered.

Commanders were called. Officials came scurrying up to the wall. All the villagers gathered at the base, peering up at the commotion. Alaren brought forth his brothers' letters in which they stated that they wouldn't move the wall an inch except into the other brother's territory.

"So," Alaren said, turning and passing his stone to the village woman as she gave hers to him, "we're invading and building new walls on either side of this village. You," he pointed to Shirar's forces, "will patrol on the east side. And you," he pointed to Marin's regiment, "will patrol on the west side."

"But who will patrol on this wall?" asked an official.

"No one," Alaren said firmly, "because we need these stones to build the new walls."

"But we're not going to move the walls!" someone protested. "We're warriors, not masons. We don't build walls!"

Alaren bit back a sigh. Warriors built terrible walls, invisible ones that divided people's hearts - but that was a comment for another day. He whistled through his fingers and the Stonemasons Guild stepped forward, tools in hand, ready to take down and rebuild the walls.

"The masons have agreed to do the work," Alaren explained, "and the villagers have agreed to house and feed them."

As you might imagine, elegant as the scheme was, the officials objected. So, one morning, after days of arguing, Alaren picked up a chisel and struck the first blow to the wall. The sound rang out like a bell. Within moments, the villagers and stonemasons ran to the wall and began to tear it down. The officials shrieked and screamed, but the warriors stood back and simply watched the villagers. They didn't particularly care which side of the village the walls stood upon. Frankly, it was a lot of bother dealing with the villagers tromping back and forth over the walls simply because they forgot their knitting basket at their mother's house.

And so, it was done. The Brothers Wall was moved, stone by stone, to either side of the village. The villagers declared themselves to be neither Shirar nor Marin's citizens, but members of Alaren's Peace Force. Their land belonged to no one. As a Peace Village, they offered sanctuary to all who could abide by their rules. Years later, when the war was coming to an end, this peace village would host the peace treaty negotiations. But that, my friends, is another story.

~ The End ~

Behind the Story - Real Life Inspiration
The Fall of the Berlin Wall

This fictional story was inspired by the tragic story of walls built along borders around the world . . . and the hopeful story of the fall of the Berlin Wall in 1989. After World War II, Berlin was divided in half when Germany was split into East and West Germany. A long, concrete divider was built through the city in 1961. Many people tried to cross the wall. 5,000 succeeded; 200 were killed.

In 1989, amidst unrest and nonviolent revolutions

throughout other nearby Soviet Bloc countries, East Germans launched a series of protests that led to the government declaring that the gates of the Berlin Wall would be opened. On November 9th, 1989, after a radio broadcast announced that the borders were opened, East Germans flocked to the wall, demanding to be let through.

The demolition of the wall began that very night by citizens chipping off pieces for souvenirs, and opening up new, unofficial border crossings. This continued over several weeks and included bulldozers breaking down the wall to reconnect divided streets that formerly ran between East and West Berlin. The fall of the Berlin Wall laid the groundwork for German reunification on October 3rd of 1990.

In Alaren's story, the people of the village used creative nonviolent action to build an alternative to the Brothers Wall. In this folktale, the building of the perimeter walls is not a perfect solution to building peace, but it meets the villagers' immediate needs of access to the two parts of their home. As with Gandhian Constructive Programme, the building of the solution quickly becomes a direct challenge to the problem. The Brothers Wall holds the stones they need to rebuild the walls in a new place. In the long run, resolving the problem of the division set the stage for deeper peace work, including the use of the town as the location for peace negotiations. This is a common pattern in peace work and change-making: small steps prepare us for larger goals.

Alaren's story also includes another important type of action: direct action and noncompliance with injustice. Alaren and the villagers refuse to bow to "authority" and accept the wall. Instead, they take tangible actions to create a solution and deconstruct the wall. They rally allies in the Stonemasons Guild and sway potential opponents of soldiers to simply stand aside and let the work of change take place. All of this helped the changes occur.

Discussion Question:

- Think of the fences in your neighborhood or community. Who put up the fences? How do these fences help or hinder your neighborhood or community?
- What would your life be like if there were no walls?
- Imagine if there were no borders. How would that change our world?

The Brothers Wall

- Alaren Clowns Around -
A Potato. A Tin Cup. A Child's Shoe.

The tension was thick. The air sizzled. Alaren could feel the danger before he heard the argument. He quickened his pace, threading through the ribbon of refugees to the army checkpoint. A pair of young soldiers shouted at the huddle of tired villagers, pointing back the way they had come. The refugees protested. They couldn't go back. There were only ruins behind them. Death was at their heels. Shirar's army was torching villages as they battled eastward.

Beyond this army checkpoint, the foothills dropped down to Mari Valley. Safety was in sight . . . if only they could pass through. The soldiers had orders, however. Fearful of spies, King Marin had ordered the border closed. The refugees were trapped in the war zone, desperate to get out.

A soldier brandished his sword, telling them not to pass. One of the refugees gripped his walking staff, preparing to fight the soldier. A nervous gasp ran through the group.

Alaren eased closer. He began to whistle a jaunty little tune, the kind the shepherds twiddled around with on their pipes when they were bored in the high pastures. He pulled a trio of apples out of his pocket - tiny, knobby things - and started to juggle them. Confusion rippled through the group. What was crazy Alaren up to now? The tall, thin man threw a wild toss and dove to catch the apple, sliding between the staff-wielding refugee and soldier.

"Does anyone have a potato?" Alaren asked, ignoring the confused looks.

After a ripple of mutters, a round potato sailed toward him. Alaren caught it and threaded it into the juggling. He glanced at the soldiers.

"Spare that tin cup a moment?" he asked, nodding at the standard-issue cup perched on the nearby fence post.

The young soldiers frowned, but then he lowered his sword from the man's nose. He tossed the cup into the arcing loop of items.

"If I can get to seven objects," Alaren wagered, watching the spinning circuit nervously, "will you let us through?"

A refugee camp was located a few miles further down the road. If the people got through this checkpoint, they could reach it by nightfall.

"Ten," the soldier countered, eyeing the thin man as he scrambled to catch the tin cup.

Alaren agreed, bent down, and scooped up a rock. He added it to his juggling. The villagers offered some of their meager belongings. Another potato, a boy's wooden ball, and a second cup joined Alaren's juggling. Nine objects whirled. An air of anticipation rose.

"One more," Alaren said at last, concentrating so hard that sweat rolled down his brow.

A little girl hopped forward and handed him her shoe. He nearly dropped everything, but with a wild lunge, he recovered, spun all the objects - three apples, two cups, a stone, two potatoes, a ball, and a shoe - thrice more. He let the stone fall to the ground, tossed the potatoes to their owners, sent the ball rolling to the boy, shot one cup to the man who lent it, lunged and placed the other back on the fence post, stuck the apples in his pocket, and handed the shoe back to the little girl with a flourish and a bow.

Cheers and applause burst out. Laughter rang against the hills.

The soldier spluttered. His face turned red. At first, he didn't want to let them through, but the other soldier told him to honor his promise.

"What will it hurt, really?" he told his fellow soldier with a shrug.

"But orders are orders," the first soldier blustered.

"Yeah? And honor is honor," the other replied. "You made a wager. You lost. Now you have to keep your part of the deal."

At last, the soldier relented. He opened the gate and let the refugees through.

"I didn't know you could juggle," the burly man who had almost gotten into a fight muttered to Alaren as they crossed through.

"Neither did I," Alaren answered with a slight smile. "The best I've ever managed before was five."

"What if you had lost?" the man asked with a frown.

Alaren shrugged. His intention had been to calm the soldiers and the crowd, avoiding the violence that threatened to break out. Whether he dropped the balls or not didn't matter as much as saving peoples' lives at that moment.

"In truth," he told the man, clapping him on the soldier, "as soon as I'd started, I'd already won."

~ The End ~

Behind the Story - Real Life Inspiration
Peace Teams

When I first heard the story of a peace team member "clowning around" at a border checkpoint in Palestine, I thought it was the craziest, most dangerous thing I'd ever heard! That was before I'd done any peace team training and before I'd learned about the contrary logic of nonviolent conflict transformation. Around the world, peace teams are made up of people who enter "hot" conflict zones to help build peace and de-escalate violence. They accompany activists and organizers to diminish the risk of assault from either side of an armed conflict. Teams in Israel and Palestine walk with Palestinian organizers as they challenge the unjust policies of Israeli occupation. Teams in Colombia provide protective witnesses for peace community organizers. In other places, I heard stories about people playing violins, telling jokes, and de-escalating tension in odd and creative ways. Once, when Civil Rights organizer Bernard Lafayette was arrested with others, they sang in jail to let the guards know they were not afraid of them. This approach won over the guards to the point that the guard ended up buying them ice cream! Can you believe that?!

When I finally took a peace team training with the Metta Center for Nonviolence, I learned about the logic and skills that these seemingly foolhardy, unarmed persons were using in the courageous work of peace teams. It turns out that if your goal is to stop violence, carrying a gun or balling your fist are not the best approaches. Such aggression often aggravates tension and leads to violence. Stress and domination tactics increase the heart rate, pump adrenaline through the veins of both the dominator and their target, and trigger the fight/flight/freeze reaction in most people. Peace teams intentionally strive to shift the dynamics of the encounter away from these responses.

Peace teams diffuse tension, ease fear with humor and creativity, humanize the individuals (vs. demonizing and dehumanizing people as suspects, targets, offenders, enemies, or criminals), and re-activate the empathy neurons of the people involved in the conflict, making them less likely to engage in violence. Peace teams shift the conflict from a place where violence seems like the only option (like in the story when the soldiers and refugees are nearly at blows) to a place where other solutions can be considered. In the fictional folktale, Alaren's goal with his juggling was to break up a brewing fight. That's why he could say he'd "already won". It was a bonus that he managed to secure the safe passage of the villagers through the checkpoint.

If you'd like to learn more about international peace teams, check out Nonviolent Peaceforce and Peace Brigades International. Here in the United States, the Meta Peace Team does this work in cities and neighborhoods, as well as at contentious protests. Another excellent resource is the documentary "The Interrupters" which tells the story of how Cease Fire Chicago brought together former gang members to form a peace team to stop gang violence in their neighborhoods.

Discussion Questions:

- Why did Alaren say that he had already won when he started the juggling, even if he was not sure he would manage with ten objects?
- What could the soldier have said if he had not managed to juggle all the objects?
- If a fight *had* broken out between the older man and the soldier, how could people have intervened and calmed it down?

- Every Man Your Brother; Every Woman Your Sister -

When soldiers come to capture refugees,
one man must choose between hate and love.

As the war intensified, many people sought refuge in the Peace Villages. Alaren's Peace Force welcomed defecting soldiers from both armies. They sheltered Border Mountain villagers whose homes had been ruined. They made room for travelers and refugees when the occupying armies blocked the roads to the lowland cities. Alaren's Peace Villages had few rules, but those he had were challenging to follow.

Anyone seeking refuge in a Peace Village had to give up their weapons like everyone else. They had to join the trainings in the Way Between and learn nonviolent ways of stopping fights and building peace. They had to take up the creed: do harm to none, be good toward all. They had to help with the chores and tasks of maintaining life. And lastly, they had to see all people as their brothers and sisters - or at least try.

Alaren watched former soldiers swallow hatred of former enemies. He saw villagers confront their gripping fear of soldiers. His Peace Force made space for stories to be shared, grief to be aired, and anger to let loose in a circle of healing. It took effort for the bile of bitterness to be transformed into the ability to allow the words *brother* and *sister* to pass through the lips of people who had fought or fled for their lives during this awful war. At times, Alaren despaired of ever succeeding, but he viewed the challenges as a necessary part of moving toward peace.

Then, one day, his efforts paid off in a way no one expected.

A new flood of refugees had just arrived at the High Rock Peace Village, one of six such communities scattered around this cluster of mountain peaks. The refugees had escaped from one of Shirar's prisoner-of-war camps, stealing away in the night and fleeing across the ridge. Warriors carried children and supported elders. Villagers hauled gravely injured warriors in slings. They had hoped to cross the contested territories into Marianan lands, but they had been ill-informed: two more mountain ridges stood between them and safety. They'd never make it before the enemy soldiers caught them. They begged for shelter and sanctuary in the Peace Village, knowing that the armies sometimes left those communities alone.

Alaren held a hasty conference. If Shirar's warriors discovered escaped prisoners among the villagers, their fragile truce with the armies would be shattered. But the villagers looked at the weary faces of women, the tear-streaked cheeks of children, the old people confronting death, the wounded, the sick . . . and their hearts were moved into courage.

They brought fresh clothes, warm blankets, and hot soup. Every scrap of identifying Marianan blue was replaced with the humble homespun tunics of the villagers. The weapons the warriors had stolen before escaping were hidden away in a cave outside the village. The refugees were split up among the houses, though some grumbled about taking in the warriors.

"Every man is your brother," Alaren reminded them all, "just as every woman is your sister."

"Not me, dearie," one of his sassier older grandmothers cackled, "these lads had best be my grandchildren. Nobody'd believe this handsome fellow's my brother."

She patted the sternest warrior on the shoulder. Everyone chuckled. Alaren thanked his lucky stars for the wisdom and humor of old women . . . his efforts for peace would never go anywhere without them.

Hardly had the last refugee been stowed away in the crowded homes when Shirar's soldiers arrived.

"We're tracking escaped prisoners," the commander announced, "and the tracks came straight to you."

"There are tracks, certainly," Alaren answered easily, "but they don't belong to your prisoners. The villagers at Low Rock have evacuated to the safety of our homes."

He pointed over the ridge where the smoke of smoldering ruins rose. There was truth to his words: they had also taken in the dozen survivors of the attack.

"How many prisoners did you lose?" Alaren asked cordially.

"More than two dozen men, women, and children," the commander answered.

"Ah, well, that's far more than we have tracks for, certainly," Alaren pointed out, gesturing to the ground. The compassion of those who had carried children or the injured on litters protected the truth of their numbers.

"All the same," the commander answered, "we'd like to search the village."

"Be my guest," Alaren invited, "but please do no harm to my villagers."

Shirar's soldiers saw children hiding their faces in their mothers' skirts. They saw sick elders huddled under the covers as their sons and daughters wiped their fevered brows. They saw husbands carrying armloads of wood to stoke the fire for their wives. Nowhere did they see anyone who bore a Marianan blue tunic as many of the escaped prisoners did.

They questioned the villagers about extra adults, but all they heard was, "Oh, that woman's my sister" or "That man's my brother".

They came to the home of a man named Jokran. Alaren held his breath. Jokran was a former soldier from Shirar's army. Of all the dwellers in the Peace Village, Jokran had given him the hardest time about using the term brother. He swore he would never call his enemies by that word; it dishonored the memory of his real brothers who had been killed in the war. He had seen them die, each struck down in turn by the same ferocious warrior. Jokran had given chase, but lost sight of the man in the heat of battle. Since coming to the peace village, Jokran had kept a tenuous peace with the deserters in the village, but he neither forgave nor forgot his brothers' deaths.

When Alaren had split up the refugees, he'd had no choice but to put one of the injured warriors in with Jokran. The man was unconscious, and Alaren hoped he'd stay that way until Shirar's soldiers were gone. As he entered, he could see the man's shirtsleeve had been rolled back. A long scar stretched from elbow to wrist on his left arm. Jokran was staring at the scar with a pale face and clenched fists.

"Who is this?" the commander asked.

Silence met his question.

Please, Alaren begged Jokran with his eyes, *please think of the children even if you hate this man. Don't give him away or you give all of us away.*

Suspicious, the commander strode forward and barked at Jokran.

"I said, who is this?!" the commander asked sharply.

"My brother!" Jokran burst out. He licked his lips nervously and swallowed hard. "This . . . this is my brother. I - I can prove it."

133

He slowly rolled back his sleeve. A long white scar stretched from wrist to elbow.

"We are blood-sworn," Jokran said in a whisper.

The answer sufficed. Later, after the soldiers had left, Alaren sought Jokran out. The man was sitting with his head in his hands at the bedside of the scarred man, eyes red with weeping.

"That isn't your brother," Alaren remarked quietly, pulling up a stool and waiting. "You told me long ago that your brothers are dead."

The story came out in pieces, as hard stories often do. Alaren listened silently, making room for the tale. Jokran had foresworn violence, except for one last fight. He had vowed to kill the Marianan soldier who had slain his blood brothers. All he knew about him was that he had a long scar on his arm. Jokran rolled back his sleeve as he spoke, revealing a similar long white scar - the mirror of the man in the bed's - on his arm.

"I gave this to myself and swore upon my brothers' graves to find the man with the matching scar. I did not know the man's name, nor could I see his face under his battle helmet, but the scar would serve to remind me of this vow."

"Why didn't you kill him, then?" Alaren asked when Jokran fell silent. "You could have given him to the soldiers and let him hang."

The other man was quiet for a long time. At last, he spoke.

"I wanted to . . . it would have been so easy. I was sitting in here, waiting, half-mad with fury at the sight of this man's scar and all it meant to me. I started thinking how strange fate is, that it delivered this man to me now. I mean, you might have put some children or one of the elders in here with me . . . but that got me thinking about them. I realized if I gave him up, the soldiers would suspect the whole village. We'd all hang."

So, when the commander asked for the bed-ridden man's identity, Jokran cried out for forgiveness to his brothers' spirits and obeyed the Peace Village's rule.

"This man is my brother," he had said . . . and a strange thing happened.

"It seemed to me that my brothers' spirits came to me as you walked the soldiers to the road," Jokran said with a choked voice, "and they told me there was a way to put their spirits at rest. I had to take this man as my brother and help him return to life. Then, I was to call in the life-debt he would owe me by asking him to join our Peace Force, to foreswear the ways of war and killing, and to repay the lives he owes me with lives saved by waging peace."

Alaren squeezed Jokran's shoulder and sat with him for a long time.

The refugees remained at High Rock Peace Village. Over the months, then years, the lies the Peace Force had told Shirar's soldiers grew into truths: orphaned children became sons and daughters, elders were included in families as mothers and fathers, women bonded with new sisters, and slowly - ever so slowly - strangers and enemies found that the words *brother* and *sister* were not so painful on their tongues. The rules of the Peace Village sounded simple at first, but following them was harder than anything an army asked of its soldiers. Those rules required a different kind of courage from them all.

~ The End ~

Behind the Story - Real Life Inspiration
A Cure for Violence and
Andre Trocmé of Le Chambon-sur-Lignon

This story is derived from two real-life stories. The first appears in Richard Attenborough's Gandhi biopic. A Hindu man approaches Gandhi and confesses that he has killed a Muslim man. He cries out that there is no hope of absolution for him for this crime. Gandhi says there is a cure. The man must find a Muslim child orphaned by the violence and raise that child as his own. But there was a catch: even though the man was Hindu, he had to raise the child to be a Muslim. This way, the Hindu man will find respect and love for Muslims, and the child will be raised to love Hindus - thus breaking the cycle of Hindu-Muslim violence.

This anecdote inspired Jokran's journey in this story. Where war and violence dehumanize people, peace and nonviolence consistently strive to build relationships and rehumanize the people involved in a bitter and deadly conflict. When his brothers' spirits tell him to make peace with his enemy, they are showing how the cycle of revenge does not necessarily bring us peace. They offer him a different way to heal.

The other story that inspired my fictional adaptation is the effort of André and Magda Trocmé (and others) in the French village of Le Chambon-sur-Lignon during WWII. André had been banished to the remote village for his pacifist views, but during the Nazi Occupation of France, he and his wife established a series of safe houses for fleeing Jews. The local villagers met the children at the train station and pretended they were simply greeting relatives. Then they enrolled the children in their schools, often right under the noses of the Nazis. When asked to produce a list of Jews, Trocmé replied, "We do not know what a Jew is. We only know men." It is estimated that between 1940-1945, the village saved the lives of 3,500-5,000 Jewish refugees.

The stories of courageous people hiding fellow humans from deadly discovery are vast and many. They crop up anywhere persecution occurs, and often cross surprising lines of bias and alliances. These tales inspire us to reach out to one another with our common humanity and use our open hearts to protect and safeguard each other.

Discussion Questions:

- Describe a time when your initial opinion of someone was changed once you got to know them.
- Why do we sometimes make assumptions about someone before we get to know them? How can this lead to stereotypes?
- Can you think of other examples where people hid other people in order to keep them safe?
- What kind of rules or guidelines could help people to build a culture of peace, like the rules of the Peace Village?

- The Witch's Hut -

How a strange old woman protected the children.

Almina was a witch, everyone knew that. And everyone left her well alone. Even the soldiers of the two warring armies of Marin and Shirar carefully skirted the tiny valley where Almina's hut and chicken coop, pig wallow and vegetable field lay. The armies attacked and plundered every other village in the area. They stole the cattle from the pastures. They trampled the turnips and carrots at the farms. But they left Almina alone for fear that she'd curse them . . . and Almina was perfectly fine with that. In fact, she fanned the flames of her reputation by spreading tall tales about toads who had once been mean old army captains and hogs that had once been rude soldiers.

The only thing she missed was the children . . . the local kids used to come play in the little brook that ran through her fields, but now, if they drew close at all, it was only to call her names and toss stones at the bones and skulls she hung on her fence to discourage unwanted visitors - like armies.

There came a day when the bitterness of war stung the soldiers into a mad frenzy of battle rage. Dual orders to take no prisoners whipped the armies into a bloodbath that massacred entire villages. Alaren's Peace Force saved as many as they could, but still the rivers ran red and the night skies blazed smoky orange with burning villages. Rumors of spies hiding amidst the Peace Force sent both armies chasing Alaren's followers over peak and canyon, ravine and wooded trails. Each of the Peace Force members shepherded a small group of people to fleeting safety. Alaren traveled with the orphans of the war.

One day, he found himself trapped between the two armies with steep trails on one side and no hiding places on the other. Desperately, his band of orphans ran up the path until they froze outside the Bone Gate in the witch's fence.

"Go! Go!" Alaren urged.

"It's the Witch's Hut!" one of the orphans cried.

"Better to be a living toad than a dead boy," Alaren told him, opening the gate and shooing the children through.

The children followed; it was better to be with Alaren than anywhere else, anyway.

Almina came out to greet them on her porch.

"What have we got here, Alaren? Supper?"

"Turn them into sacks of grain and hogs and hens to hide them," Alaren urged swiftly, glancing anxiously over his shoulder, "because the bloodthirsty soldiers are on our tails and we've nowhere left to hide."

Almina had a root cellar. She put four children in it underneath a stack of potato sacks. Almina had an attic. She put six children up under the eaves with bundles of drying herbs hiding them from sight. Almina had a feather bed. She put three girls under the mattress and fluffed the lumps from sight. Almina put two boys in the chicken coop rafters and two more in the dark corners of the pigsty. When she got to Alaren, they could see the soldiers swarming up the path.

"Quick, fold your stork limbs into that big iron pot. Pretend I'm cooking you," Almina hissed as a pack of men broke off from the rest and charged up the path toward the house.

The witch roughed her tidy bun into a wild bird's nest and flung the front door open, startling the soldiers. Her eyes rolled in different directions. Her limbs convulsed. Gibberish poured from her lips.

"Be gone! Unless you're here to be my supper, be off with you!" she cackled madly.

They could see a man inside an iron pot screaming and cursing and trying to break the invisible magic spell that bound him in place in the Witch's Pot.

"Be gone!" Almina warned. "Take your swords and armies with you. I'll put poxes on your backsides, boils on your noses, and make you all see double as your tongues tie into knots."

"Why shouldn't I just kill you?" a soldier threatened.

"He who kills the Witch will die within a fortnight," she intoned, "but his spirit will never rest. He will starve, but be unable to eat. Thirst, but never be able to drink. Water, wine, ale: all will pour straight through him. His son's sons' sons unto the thirteenth generation will be driven mad by voices no one else can hear. His daughters will be ugly as demons and birth monsters unto the end of time."

Almina frankly thought she was overdoing it, but the soldiers stepped back a pace and then another. Not far enough though, so Almina grabbed an old bucket and a stick and banged on them with all the ferocity she could muster. She was just one woman with more age than youth under her belt, but by her bones, she'd do her best to run those soldiers off!

She invented curses and spells as fast as she could breathe. She drooled and spat. She shook her limbs and howled. At last, she started to tear off her clothes like a madwoman.

With a look of horror, the young soldiers fled. They grabbed their fighting companions and stammered about a witch's curse, hauling them back as they pointed in fear to the house. Almina turned, puzzled by that reaction. She bit back her laughter at the sight she saw. Alaren had hissed instructions to the children in the attic. They seized the rafters and shook until the whole house trembled like a living beast. The orphans hidden in the outbuildings did the same. The pigs and chickens came out squealing and squawking. The commotion grew so great that it looked like Almina had brought her house to life like a snarling, enormous guard dog.

The tales of the cursed Witch's Hut spread far and wide, growing wilder with each retelling. No soldier ever stepped beyond the Bone Gate again. As the war raged on, Alaren brought children from all over the Border Mountains to hide with the witch.

And that is why every child knows that beneath the rumors of a horrible witch lies a friendly old crone ready to make magic and go mad to save the lives of children.

~ The End ~

Behind the Story - Real Life Inspiration
Zula Karuhimbi, the Rwandan Healer Who Saved Lives Through "Sorcery" and Courage

This story is inspired by the real-life example of Zula Karuhimbi, a traditional Rwandan healer. In 1996, when the Hutus rose up against the Tutsis in what became known as the Rwandan Genocide, Zula Karuhimbi rose up into action to protect people. Over the 100-day period, she hid more than 150 people in and around her house. Some she hid in a pit in the backyard. Once she hid twenty people in the crawl space under her roof. She even put people under her bed. Then she raced to the front door to confront the machete and gun-armed Hutus. She would rub the stinging juices of plants on her hands and touch their arms; welts would appear, giving rise to rumors that she was a witch who would use sorcery against them. Despite her diminutive size, she would grab anything at hand and make a loud racket, banging pots and pans, yelling and shouting in gibberish . . . anything to surprise the attackers into leaving her - and her hidden refugees - alone. Even when her own children were murdered, she persisted in trying to help others. People said she was mad or a witch, but by the end of the genocide, almost everyone who had sought refuge with her had survived.

In an interview in 2014, she said that, even after witnessing the horrors of the genocide, there was only one real thing that mattered in life: love.

"Love is the most important thing," she said. "Find someone to love and the future will always be bright."

Discussion Questions:

- Would you be willing to hide people in your home if they were in danger?
- This tactic worked in real life and in the story because people believed in witches. What are some things that people believe in your culture that could be used in the same way?

- Questions That Save Lives -
How Alaren stops a soldier from attacking a school.

A war zone is no place for a child, but when war breaks out around them, what are children to do?

Alaren is known as a great friend to the children. He had that way about him, a kind of quiet and silliness that drew children to him. He never bossed them around, he listened deeply, and he played fun games. He openly and eagerly learned from his young friends and that inspired their trust in him.

Sadly, Alaren also watched many of his young friends die, not just from the battles of war, but from the hunger and diseases that followed war like a pack of wolves. Even more became orphans when their parents perished.

During the insanity of the Brothers War, when the fighting sides hit a peak of senselessness and desperation, massacres turned the Border Mountains red. After an encounter with a mad soldier - a young man with nothing left but war cries in his voice and bloodlust in his eyes - a frightened traveler ran to the nearby village to warn them of the man's approach. Not knowing if the man was alone or with a squadron of soldiers, the villagers evacuated at once, climbing the hills to a set of hidden caves. One woman, however, ran back out and screamed.

"The children! The children are still at the school!"

Alaren was visiting at that time and he raced back down the slope through the empty village. His heart thundered and ached all at once. That school had been a bright spot in a long, dark war. It had stayed open, day after day, while other village schools burned or shut down due to attacks. It was a simple, one-room building on the edge of the cluster of houses.

When he drew close, Alaren skidded to a stop. The teacher had barred the door and locked the inside window shutters. Outside, the mad soldier hurled his weight against the heavy wooden door, again and again. A roar erupted from his throat. His sword was clenched in one fist. A feverish look burned in his eyes. He was young, very young.

In another time, Alaren thought with surreal clarity, *that soldier would be in that school, still at his lessons.*

That's how young the boy was.

Alaren had seen this sort of madness before. It was a toxic blend of terror, rage, pain, and panic. It clouded the minds of soldiers young and old, but the youths got it the worst. It struck in the heat of fighting or the dead of night when the ballads and legends of heroic battles turned into the terrifying nightmares of war's reality. The panicked madness, once started, was hard to stop. Attacking the youth would only deepen it. Trying to restrain him in a bear hug would trigger a violent terror in the boy. Shouts and loud noises worsened the paranoia. Reason and logic wouldn't cut through the fog of its delusions. Alaren cast around and saw a drawn bucket of well water with a ladle inside, abandoned when the villagers fled.

"Thirsty work, breaking in a door," Alaren remarked softly, picking up the bucket and offering out a ladleful.

The boy whirled. Alaren made ready to run. For a long tense moment, neither moved or spoke. The boy had lifted his sword, wary.

"What's your favorite dessert?" Alaren asked, calmly sipping the well water then offering it to the youth again.

The young soldier blinked in confusion. His chest heaved. His eyes focused on Alaren, slowly.

"Dessert?" he repeated in an uncertain tone.

"Pie? Spice cake? I enjoy a nice bread pudding, myself, or gingerbread on a snowy night." He eyed the boy. "You look like a toffee fan."

"Fudge," the youth said in a strange, wistful tone, as if his thoughts had suddenly flown miles away and back through time.

Alaren didn't quite know what to do next, only that he had to keep the youth talking instead of breaking down that door.

"Take a drink," Alaren invited gently, "and rest a bit."

The youth didn't move any closer, but his sword lowered an inch.

"Is your home in a small village like this?" Alaren asked, gesturing around.

The youth shook his head. He had been born and raised in a city.

"It's rough, seeing war," Alaren murmured. "We all get weary of it, don't we? I'm tired of it, wish it would end. Don't you get tired, too?"

The youth blinked and nodded.

"The other day, I was ready to die," Alaren confessed. "It was just too much. A very rough day, full of very sad things. There was so much death and perhaps I shouldered more sorrow than was my share. Have you ever felt like that?"

Alaren just kept going, the words flowing out of him in a gentle tone. Inch-by-inch, the boy's sword began to lower. He told the youth that it would be alright, he'd get out of this war, peace would come, he'd go home, heal, things would change.

All at once, the youth shuddered from head to toe and his words burst out of him like a chick from an egg, raw and unformed. Time may have forgotten the exact words of the young soldier's story, but we can guess at the pain of a boy who should be in school, but was sent to fight instead. We can imagine the horrible things he witnessed and the terrible violence he had done. We can envision the mad grief and fear that drove him to that village. Time has forgotten his words, but it remembers what Alaren did: the older man convinced the boy to put down his sword and meet the villagers he had come to kill.

"But won't they hate me?" the youth cried.

Alaren shrugged slightly.

"Perhaps . . . but perhaps not. After all, you could have killed their children and instead you stopped to have a drink of water and a conversation with me. That choice is where all peace - yours, mine, theirs - begins."

Alaren could be quite persuasive when he needed to be . . . and before the day was out, he had invited the young soldier to lay down his sword and pick up the ways of peace. For decades, the young man would tell the story about how he came to end life and instead found a chance for life among the people who worked for peace.

~ The End ~

Behind the Story - Real Life Inspiration
Antoinette Tuff Stops a School Shooter

In 2013, Antoinette Tuff was filling in for a coworker at an elementary school in DeKalb County, Georgia, when twenty-year-old Michael Brandon Hill walked in with an automatic assault rifle and 500 rounds of ammunition. She wound up stuck in the same room as him as the school went on lockdown. After a period of terror, she blurted out an absurd question, "May I go to the bathroom?"

He said yes. As she rose to leave, she realized that he was also going into the hall. Even though she thought she might be able to get away, she realized that the shooter might go and find the children. So, she paused. Turning back into the room, she called him back from the doorway. The police were on the scene, surrounding the building and preparing to shoot the young man.

Gently, lovingly (and filled with a strange sense of calm) she said, "Sweetheart, come back in here. Bullets don't have no names. And those bullets gonna kill me and you. I need you to come back in here and it's gonna be you and me and we will work this thing out."

Antoinette spoke with him for hours, relating how everyone had bad days - she had struggled with suicidal urges that year - and encouraged him to put down the gun and surrender to the police. At last, that's exactly what happened. This is one of the few times a school shooter has been apprehended instead of shot. Antoinette Tuff's nonviolent response managed to stop Michael Brandon Hill before he killed any children and even saved his own life.

Conflict researchers identified several important violence de-escalation tactics in what she did: she interrupted the victim/persecutor cycle with an unusual question (asking to go to the bathroom). She built empathy with the young man. She remained calm and did not escalate his tension. She talked to him with compassion until he was willing to find a way out of the situation without killing anyone.

The researchers are careful to note that there is no formula for these encounters, that these same tactics might not work in another situation. However, these approaches are part of the tools that we all should know. You never know when they might save lives . . . including your own.

Discussion Questions:

* What surprised you about these stories (both real and fiction)?
* What would inspire you to do something like what Antoinette Tuff or Alaren did?
* Have you ever stood up for someone who needed your help, even if it was risky or dangerous?

-Enemies Take Lives; Friends Save Them -
Once, they were enemies. Now, they are allies for peace.

Alaren's Peace Force grew by the hour, it seemed. His peace villages drew refugees seeking shelter. The relief efforts engaged thousands. At a certain point during the Brothers War, the casualties were so great and the doctors so few, that Alaren set up a hospital on the edge of the battlefield and started treating mortal enemies side-by-side. These were mad and wild times when waking hours turned to nightmares and sleep was little more than a dream. It was in the hospital that Alaren first devised the white tunics with the Mark of Peace. The first ones were nothing more than capes made of his peace flags that kept his medic teams from being killed.

Soon, the sight of a white tunic with a black ink circle of interlocking patterns of sand dunes and water ripples gave the wearer amnesty and a slim margin of protection in the war zone. Alaren convinced many recovering warriors to trade in blue or red tunics in favor of a white one as they healed within his makeshift hospital. It's hard to deny the request for peace from someone who has just saved your life.

While the stories about Alaren's Peace Force are many, this particular story is about two of Alaren's recruits, Bokli and Markle, warriors from opposite sides of the conflict who lay on the edge of death in two cots beside each other in Alaren's hospital.

"If I live," Bokli prayed to the dry ancestor wind, "I will wage peace instead of war."

"If I live," Markle vowed to the ever-flowing ancestor river, "I will lay down the sword and spend the rest of my life making sure no one ever picks up a weapon again!"

Alaren heard their fevered murmurs and swore by the Way Between that he would hold them to their promises. As they recovered, Alaren plied them for their stories. From those stories grew conversations and, by the time the two former enemies rose to their feet, they rose as friends.

Alaren put them through the training all members of his Peace Force took. Then they went into the field as a pair, wearing the white tunics over their strapping warrior frames. They lived in one of the Peace Villages. When the armies came to attack or raid, the pair would run to the gate and block it with their arms held wide open to show they had no weapons. If it were Shirar's soldiers, Bokli would tell his kinsmen not to kill a fellow desert man over a few scrawny chickens and a village of peace-loving children. If it were Marin's soldiers, Markle would step forward and sadly say that the price for attacking the village would be his life, a good Marianan life. Was it worth making a widow out of his wife and a fatherless son out of his boy?

All through the war, Bokli and Markle protected the village by putting their courage in the path of harm. When the war ended, the two parted ways just long enough to ask their families to move to the village with them.

Thus, Alaren turned enemies into friends, and friends into peace's protection, and peace into the future of families.

~ The End ~

Behind the Story - Real Life Inspiration
Unarmed Peacekeepers in South Sudan Save Lives

In 2013, unarmed peacekeepers Derek Oakley and his colleague Andres Gutierrez were serving in South Sudan. Their role was to offer protective accompaniment to people living in the conflict-riddled area. One day, soldiers invaded a protective encampment and killed 58 people. Derek and Andres ran into a building and sheltered five women and nine children using nonviolent training to survive repeated threats with guns, axes, and sticks. They refused an order to leave the women and children behind. Derek and Andres knew that if they left, the others would be killed. Instead, they stayed, calmly insisting that these innocent people had nothing to do with the war.

Their intervention saved the lives of the people in the building - and possibly their own. Their story inspired my story of Bokli and Merkle's choices to intervene on behalf of villagers when their fellow soldiers came to attack. There are many stories of courageous, nonviolent interventions like this. They are hair-raising, inspiring, and eye-opening. You can find out more by looking up Nonviolent Peaceforce.

This story also draws inspiration from Veterans For Peace. Like Bokli and Merkle, these are war veterans who renounce war and devote their lives to peace. In the United States and internationally, the Veterans For Peace are an active group that opposes war, militarism, the military-industrial complex, nuclear weapons, drone strikes and much more.

Discussion Questions:

- Would you consider participating in an unarmed peacekeeping training? Why or why not?
- What about a neighborhood peace team training? Or an anti-bully training?

- The Taste of Love -
*In the midst of war, how could anyone
remember what love was like?*

The war dragged on. The Border Mountains seethed with
danger. Refugees flooded east and west into the cities of the
river valley and the towns of the desert. Plague stalked the
villages, growing out of rotting corpses. Each army harassed
supply wagons and caravans. Hungry soldiers raided even
hungrier villages. Both sides insisted that enemy soldiers were
hiding in the villagers' thatched houses. One by one, they burnt
the dwellings to the ground.

Alaren and his Peace Force traveled up and down the war
zone, helping refugees, healing the wounded and the sick, and
rebuilding houses before the winter storms came howling down
from the peaks. There was always more to be done than hands
to do it. Even at Summer Solstice, there were not enough hours
in the day to accomplish the mountain of tasks in front of them.
It seemed that as fast as they built shelters, another village was
burned. As soon as one person healed, another sick or injured
body took their cot in the sickrooms. Some days it seemed
impossible; the combined destruction of both armies created
chaos and suffering that no army of peace, no matter how great,
could alleviate. At such times, despair choked the hearts of
Alaren's friends and followers. But Alaren never seemed to lose
hope.

One day, they turned to him and asked him for his secret.

"How is it that you never lose hope?" they asked.

Alaren offered a small smile.

"Hope in what?" he replied. "Hope that my brothers will come to their senses? I don't have to hope for that. They will, eventually. Hope that their soldiers will refuse to fight? Some are already deserting. Hope that one day a miracle will simply stop this war? No miracle will do that, but we will, one day."

He stirred the large pot of stew he was making for the new refugees.

"I never lose hope in these things because I don't squander my hope on them. Instead, I root it in things I can do with my hands. I hope this soup is at least warm and possibly tasty."

Alaren blew on a ladleful of soup and sipped it.

"But Alaren," they protested, "we're losing ground."

Every day, another village burned, another child starved, another battlefield was strewn with bodies.

"In a few moments," Alaren replied, "I will ring the bell and call people to supper. It's not much - a bowl of broth, a scrap of bread - but it comes with the most important ingredient . . . love."

He had looked into the eyes of the refugees. He had seen their despair, fear, and shock. He knew they had seen the worst of humanity. He and his followers could not right all the wrongs in the world; they had no magic wands to make all the troubles go away. But they had one miracle they could work, over and over again: they could remind people of kindness, love, and respect. His followers of the Way Between could not do everything, but anything they could do, they would . . . and they would do it with love.

"If I hope for anything," Alaren said quietly, "it is that love survives the horror of this war. I hope that the children who live through these nightmarish times will also remember that someone cared enough to make them soup and build them shelter and say that the war is wrong."

He was working to keep love alive through the war, to make sure it survived in the next generation. For if the children never saw love, if they only saw death and destruction and hate, then what other kind of world could ever come to pass? How would this nightmare ever give way to dreams?

He could place his hope in something as immediate as the kindness of a bowl of soup. He could hope that his example would remind people that love was still possible. He knew this sort of hope could take root in peoples' hearts and grow into a reality.

Alaren stirred the soup once more. Then he rang the dinner bell and called everyone to come remember the taste of love.

~ The End ~

Behind the Story - Real Life Inspiration
Lotus In A Sea of Fire

This story is based on something the Buddhist monk Thich Nhat Hanh wrote about his efforts (with others) to end the Vietnam War. It was incredibly dangerous. Both sides of the war were killing peace activists. Many of Thich Nhat Hanh's colleagues and friends died working for peace. When people criticized him for not succeeding in stopping the war, Thich Nhat Hanh replied that his goal wasn't just to stop the war. His goal was to make sure love survived the horrors of war.

He was thinking about the children who would only remember the terrors and atrocities. He recognized that if the nation were to heal in the wake of such tragedy, someone would have to demonstrate human kindness. In their work for peace, the monks and nuns rebuilt villages. They distributed food. They set up hospitals that treated everyone, no matter which side of the war they were on. With all of this, Thich Nhat Hanh and his friends were planting the seeds of loving-kindness. They were reminding their fellow humans that human decency still existed.

You can learn more about this in Thich Nhat Hanh's writings. The book in which he wrote about this in *Vietnam: Lotus in a Sea of Fire.*

Discussion Questions:

- How can you introduce more love into your school, home, and community?
- Alaren's love was in the soup he made and the homes he rebuilt. Where would you put your love? What shape would it take?

- The Shield of Love -
They had only their love.

The Brothers War went on . . . and on . . . and on. The number of graves grew. The number of warriors dwindled. The two kings, Marin and Shirar, both started conscripting people into the army, sometimes just snatching them off the street. They grabbed people from their own lands and from the war zone in the mountains. The Border Mountain villagers protested this; they wanted nothing to do with this war!

No one knew who owned their region - that was the whole point of the war, after all. Alaren was supposed to make his kingdom here, but he refused to claim a territory. So now, Kings Marin and Shirar each claimed that the Border Mountains belonged to him.

And both armies tried to snatch the Border Mountains village men and force them to fight. They did not go willingly . . . or easily. The men hid in the hills. The women refused to say where they'd gone. A code of silence rose up among the Border Mountains villagers. Sweetheart vows included the promise to not betray a lover even under torture. These were dark times, indeed.

No one resisted the taking of the men more fiercely than their mothers.

"We did not raise our sons to die in the kings' quarrel," they said hotly.

Despite their efforts, a time came to pass when a group of sons hiding in the high peaks were caught by Shirar's army. They were stuffed into red tunics and handed weapons.

"Like lambs to a slaughterhouse," the mothers wailed.

The mothers refused to give up. They haunted the army camp, protesting. They blocked the road as the soldiers marched off to war. They helped two youths desert the army. They chanted slogans at the commanders every time they set foot outside their tents, shouting, "Not our war! Not our sons!"

The mothers showed incredible courage, right down to marching onto a battlefield as a "shield of love", forming a wall of soft, round bodies in front of their strong, young sons, and refusing to let them charge down the slope to their deaths.

"This is not our war," the mothers insisted. "Why should our sons fight in it?"

"We will neither kill nor be killed for this war," the sons stated.

The situation boiled hot with tension. One of the commanders threatened to execute the mothers. The sons raised an uproar. Surprisingly, a number of other soldiers supported them. Killing enemies was one thing; murdering a bunch of old women who just wanted their sons back was another.

Amidst the conflict, Alaren proposed a compromise: let the young men join his Peace Force to work in the hospitals caring for wounded warriors. The commanders wanted to refuse, but the mothers rose such a fuss that the commanders finally agreed.

For centuries afterward, the phrase "to lift the shield of love" meant to object to one's son or daughter serving in the army. It is impossible to estimate how many lives were saved and wars averted because of mothers who wielded no swords, but instead raised up this powerful shield of love.

~ The End ~

Behind the Story - Real Life Inspiration
The Shield Of Love Demands End To Conscription

Conscription is involuntary service in the military, and, unfortunately, the world has numerous examples of this. This fictional story of mothers standing in front of their sons as a "shield of love" was inspired by the real-life "Shield of Love" made of parents of conscripts during the civil war in Yugoslavia in 1991. In real life, the parents did not stand in front of their sons directly. Instead, they organized mass demonstrations and disruptive actions in government offices.

During the civil war, parents from Bosnia-Herzegovina, Croatia, Macedonia, and Serbia protested the forced conscription of their sons into the Yugoslav People's Army. In Sarajevo, 10,000 mothers and fathers disrupted an assembly meeting, blocked traffic, and asked the governor to let them into the meetings. Several hundred parents occupied the building. The next day, they blocked traffic again and demanded - and received - buses to take them to Belgrade so they could present their demands before the Secretary of Defense.

The protests spread to other cities, government buildings, and offices of the military. Thousands of parents joined in. After a while, most branches of the Yugoslav People's Army stopped drafting new conscripts, but sons who had completed their years of service were still not released. The parents took their complaints to an international level, traveling to the European Union to protest. They waved peace flags and chanted. They held candlelight vigils. And here, the name "Shield of Love" emerged. Organized activities continued in many of the countries that made up Yugoslavia. Eventually, most of the conscripts were released.

Discussion Questions:

- What would you do to resist being forced to serve in the military?
- Would you be willing to help others resist? How would you do that?

- Stopping War -

All wars come to an end . . . eventually. After ten years of horrific battles, attacks, and raids, Alaren's efforts for peace gained traction. More and more people wanted an end to the war. In a series of campaigns, Alaren and his allies slowed, stalled, and finally stopped the war. Here are those stories.

- The Women's Day Off -
Mothers, sisters, daughters, and wives
refuse to work for war.

There came a time when the war dragged its feet and it looked like sheer inertia would bring it to an end. But Shirar had other plans. He wanted to launch a spring offensive. Through the winter, he inflamed hatred by spreading vicious rumors among his people about the Marianans.

Hearing about this, Alaren requested a meeting with his brother and was met instead by Shirar's wife. She had been sent to tell Alaren to go away - politely, of course. Tarra was as smart as she was beautiful. Alaren often wished she was in charge instead of his hot-headed brother.

"How are you, sister-in-law?" he asked as she poured him some tea.

No matter how bitterly the brothers quarreled, Tarra steadfastly showed them all basic respect and hospitality, calculating that the war would end one day and her actions would help soothe the way toward peace. She sent birthday gifts to Marin's children and never failed to inquire after Alaren's wife and family.

"Oh, about as well as can be expected," she sighed, staring out the window to where the warriors were preparing for war. She stiffened at the sight of a young boy falling to his drill partner's attack. She bit her lower lip and looked like she was about to burst into tears.

"Whatever is the matter?" Alaren asked in concern.

"Nothing, nothing," she protested. Then she hesitated. "It's just . . . Shirar sent our oldest boy to train with the warriors - and he's just a child!"

"No mother likes seeing her sons train for war," Alaren replied sorrowfully. "And she likes seeing them fight in those wars even less."

At that, Tarra burst into sobs.

"That's j-just it!" she cried. "If Marin and Shirar's war keeps going, my son will die in it."

"And many other mothers' sons, I'm afraid," Alaren agreed.

"I told Shirar that he couldn't take our son to the battlefield, not so young! But my husband told me it's none of my business - can you imagine? I'm the boy's mother! And there's nothing I can do to stop him."

"Oh, I wouldn't agree with that," Alaren commented with an amused expression.

Tarra turned to her brother-in-law. A glimmer of hope shone in her tearful eyes.

"What can I do?" she wailed. "I am just one woman."

Alaren spoke quietly of the many mothers like Tarra in the villages, towns, and cities. He told stories of grieving wives and mourning sisters, worried family members, and frightened refugees.

"You are just one woman, yes," Alaren conceded, "but you are a queen, and Shirar's wife. You can stop this war before your son ever reaches the battlefield."

He told her swiftly how she could do this. When she looked doubtful, he said, "You can save not just your son, but your nephews and your people's sons."

"Shirar will be mad as donkey sitting on a cactus!" she protested.

"Which do you want?" Alaren asked pointedly. "Your husband angry? Or your son dead?"

That settled it. Queen Tarra agreed to the plan.

A week later, the women throughout desert ceased working. They wouldn't cook. They wouldn't open up shops. They wouldn't sew or spin or weave. They wouldn't buy or sell or lend money. They wouldn't work in the fields or even tend to the children. They refused to do anything. When Shirar asked Tarra to pass him the salt at the breakfast table, she refused.

"I'm taking the day off," she answered, "and spending it with my son, whom you and Marin are about to murder in your war."

Shirar rolled his eyes and rang for the servant girl. No one came. He hollered for his manservant instead.

"Where is our serving girl?" he demanded.

"She's taken the day off, sir. She says she needs to spend time with her husband and son before they leave for battle."

Shirar was many things - greedy, hot-tempered, rash - but he wasn't stupid. He asked his manservant just how many women were taking the day off.

"All of them, sir."

Shirar's eyes bulged out.

"You mean to tell me that half my staff - "

"It's not just here, sir," the manservant added uncomfortably. "All the women in the city have stopped working and we've heard rumors that it's spreading to the desert villages and hill folk. Plenty of men have stopped work, too, sir. The women are begging them to stay home and, er, in their arms."

Shirar scowled.

"Give the women their day," he grumbled, "but tell the men that the army marches out the day after tomorrow."

But when the morning came, the men - great warriors that they were - showed up in disarray, late, only half-packed, or they didn't turn up at all.

"I couldn't just leave my children crying with my wife nowhere to be found," explained one man when his superior officer came looking for him.

"We haven't any dry clothes," another protested, pointing to the dripping wash hung on the line, "my wife left them to soak two days ago and refused to take them out."

"The mistress of horse and half the stable hands aren't here," cried a frustrated cavalry officer. "We're trying to ready the horses, but we're short of hands."

"Our chief commissions and supplies officer is a lady, and she's got the lists, and we don't know where she went!" an underling clerk wept. "We're a mess without her. We can't possibly leave today."

On and on came the excuse, explanations, delays, problems, messes, and troubles. Shirar grew red in the face and stormed to his wife's sitting room.

"Alright!" he bellowed. "What do you want?"

Shirar, remember, was no fool; he knew exactly who had organized the women's revolt. Tarra looked back at him silently, a firm and determined expression on her face.

"An end to this war, Shirar, before our son is killed in it."

"You want your precious boy?" Shirar thundered. "Fine, have him! When we march to the front, he can stay home and cower behind your skirts!"

Tarra laughed softly.

"A week ago, my dear, that would have sufficed," she answered sternly, "but I've had a bit of time to think things

167

through now."

She smiled in a way that made Shirar more nervous than facing Marin's entire army sword-less, bare-naked, and with one hand tied behind his back.

"I want all of our boys, I'm afraid, and all of our men, and what's more," she held up her hand to stop Shirar's yelling, "I want Marin's men home safe, too. Go make peace with your brother, Shirar, or you'll get no peace from me."

Nor would he get any help from the women, she warned. For they refused to lift a finger, sell a turnip, saddle a horse, cook a meal, wash a uniform, pack a sack, or anything else that would help the army send their sons, husbands, brothers, and fathers to death.

It took two weeks. Shirar tried to organize the men into action, but the rest of his country was in chaos. Without the women's help, he didn't have enough men to tend the fields, grind the grain, look after the children, care for the elders, and fight with Marin.

"If Marin marches in here and kills us all, this will be your fault," he told Tarra bitterly as he sent a messenger hawk to his brother requesting peace talks.

Tarra hid her smile. Marin wasn't going to invade. She happened to know that Alaren was headed to Marin's river valley kingdom . . . and Marin would soon have troubles enough of his own.

~ The End ~

Behind the Story - Real Life Inspiration
Icelandic Women's Strike

When women choose to withhold their participation in the "work" of society, the world literally stands still. One of the best illustrative stories of this happened in 1975 when ninety percent of the women in Iceland took "a day off" in protest over lack of equal pay for women.

Refusing to work, care for children, shop, or tend the home, the women left those tasks to the men. In the capital city, 25,000 women participated in a mass demonstration - an enormous number considering the total population of Iceland was only 220,000. The men could barely cope. Sausages (the equivalent of take-out pizza) sold out in the shops. There was no telephone service. Newspapers couldn't print because the typesetters were women. Theaters shut down when the actresses refused to perform. Bank executives had to come to the front desk and literally make change because their female tellers were absent.

By the following year, Iceland's parliament passed a law guaranteeing equal rights to women and men.

The story of the Icelandic Women's Strike reminds us where our collective power lies. As John Lennon said, "War is over, if you want it." If we wish to see an end to war - or any injustice - we need to organize our friends and neighbors in mass numbers to refuse to work or shop or keep the gears of our world turning until our demands for justice have been met. This is the basis of people power.

Discussion Questions:

- Can you imagine a women's strike in your community or nation? What would the strike demand?
- How would you - and others - go about organizing a large strike like this?
- Besides women, what are some other large groups that could take mass action together?

- The Playhouse Strike -
The Theater District doesn't find war entertaining.

On the west side of the Mari River, across from Marin's royal house, stood a row of playhouses. The theaters towered three stories tall and served as one of the cultural hubs of the nation. During the summer festivals, audience members packed the seats every evening. Colorful characters - both on stage and off - filled the area. Back then, players were not limited to traveling shows, but spent their lives in the Playhouse District, putting on one performance after another. People longing for a life in the theater flocked to the city like migrating birds and set up a veritable colony of performers, directors, writers, stagehands, set makers, and costume designers. Artists vied to paint the backdrops. Musicians composed music for each play that opened. Dancers, acrobats, magicians, and puppeteers poured their considerable talents into spectacular performances, week after week.

The theaters offered ways for people to learn new skills and train for creative professions. The playhouses took many young people under their wings in apprenticeships. The theatrical arts were considered a fine calling for a youth. Hundreds came to the island each year chasing - and often finding - their dreams.

From the outset, the young players opposed the Brothers War. They supported Alaren's call to restore the Whole World and mounted numerous plays bearing that message. They created skits and comedy acts poking fun at the nonsense of dividing the world. They featured caricatures of the kings as squabbling children in diapers fighting over toys. When the war began, they staged tragedies and true stories from the front lines, turning the numbers of deaths into a heart-wrenching plea for peace.

Marin was not amused by this. He issued an edict shutting down the theaters, but the uproar among his people forced him to rescind the order and re-open the theater district. Instead, he arrested the loudest and most prominent of the protesting playwrights. They continued to resist, smuggling scripts out of prison. Finally, as the war escalated, he decided to conscript the youths for soldiers. That would solve the problem of their treasonous anti-war plays!

Or so he thought.

Conscripting the players was like herding kittens. Even the few that Marin managed to round up caused so much trouble that they were either imprisoned or discharged. Putting humorous and dramatic anti-war storytellers in the midst of dispirited soldiers was like holding a match to a pile of dry kindling. Mutinies broke out. Desertion rates leapt up like sparks. Commanders reported that their troops laughed at them the moment their backs were turned; the players were satirizing and mimicking their mannerisms, making everyone laugh.

So, King Marin reversed his stance and banned the players from the army. The Playhouse District doubled in population. Mothers sent their sons to the stage instead of to the battlefield. And who could blame them?

During the month between the end of spring planting and the beginning of summer harvests, the Playhouse District traditionally held a massive festival. Each playhouse performed five to ten shows each day. It was a *feast* of theater that drew people from all over Mari Valley. Marin had commissioned new works about the glory of war, but that spring, Alaren journeyed to the Playhouse District. He slipped from playhouse to playhouse talking to the players. When the summer festival opened to teeming crowds, people were in for a shock.

Every playhouse in the district refused to perform war shows while the sons and daughters of the people were being killed. They went on strike and closed the highly-anticipated shows. Instead, they opened the theaters for a time of mourning and protest.

During the Playhouse Strike, as it came to be known, thousands of people took to the street to protest the war. Alaren and the followers of the Way Between conducted planning and strategy meetings in the playhouses. They trained the crowds in the Way Between. They warned Marin and Shirar by messenger hawk that the people would not support the war any longer.

Marin retaliated by burning the Playhouse District to the ground and forbidding players to own or operate theaters. It was too late to stop the opposition to the war, however. The flames of resistance spread like wildfire from the western shore of the river through the villages.

The Playhouse Strike marked a turning point in the long struggle to end the Brothers War. Marin's people refused to escalate or prolong the war. Peace was almost in sight. All that was needed was a ceasefire in the Border Mountains. The players had turned the tide . . . and that was worth the price of losing their playhouses.

In the following centuries, many kings and queens tried to buy the players' loyalties by promising theaters in exchange for supporting their wars. Some agreed; more refused. The

Playhouse District was never rebuilt, though a plaque was placed on the ruins to remind people of the sacrifice the players made to stop the war. To this day, the players wander. And to this day, the players keep their freedom to speak out against war.

~ The End ~

Behind the Story - Real Life Inspiration
Czechoslovakia's Velvet Revolution and Theater Strike

In 1989, an eruption of mass protests against the Communist regime swept through Czechoslovakia. Many civic and professional groups joined the protests and general strikes that became known as the Velvet Revolution. Among them were the theater, television, and radio professionals. Theater districts shut down shows and held open meetings instead. Dissident playwright Vaclav Havel helped establish the Civic Forum, which called for the dismissal of top officials responsible for brutalities, the release of all political prisoners, and political and economic reforms. Ten days later, new officials were appointed and the Communist government leaders resigned. In late December, Vaclav Havel was elected president.

This story served as an inspiration for Alaren's folktale about the role of the players in opposing war. All of our professional groups have collective power that can be wielded on behalf of peace and justice. Theater people and artists, especially, have played dramatic and powerful roles in many movements around the world. The anti-war songs of the '60s, Bertolt Brecht's play *Mother Courage and Her Children*, and

175

Picasso's *Guernica* are all good examples of the powerful role of the arts in the peace and anti-war movement.

A folktale about theater and resistance also offers us the chance to examine how we're each using our "stage" to speak up . . . or not. Are we remaining silent or following rote lines when grave injustices are taking place? Or are we courageously going off-script to speak from our hearts? In Alaren's folktale, the players take a courageous - and effective - stand that sets the stage for the rise of a powerful peace movement and an end to the terrible war.

Discussion Questions:

- What are some ways that the entertainment industry (movies, books, television, music, radio, Internet) supports either war or peace?
- In Alaren's tale, the theaters refuse to provide entertainment while people are dying in war. Imagine if Hollywood went on strike against war. What would this look like? Who might be involved? Do you think it could help stop our current war(s)?

The Playhouse Strike

- Alaren and the Feast Day Ceasefire -
What will it take to make peace?

Winter Solstice. The longest night of the year hung over the armies like a tomb shroud. The last glimmer of the pale sun had set behind the snow-capped peaks hours ago. The warriors huddled behind the crests and shoulders of snowy hills, trying to stay warm, despairing of seeing sunrise. No one dared light a fire for fear that a cloud of enemy arrows would rain down upon them.

"What I wouldn't give for a pint of hot cider," one grizzled warrior muttered on the east side of the hill, his blue tunic of Marin black with grime.

On the opposite side of the hill, a battle-scarred man in the red jacket of Shirar's army was thinking almost the same thing.

"What I wouldn't give to hold my wife, warm and close," he said with a shiver.

The breaths of both men turned white and rose on the air like incense ribbons burning in a temple. Alaren stood on the edge of the hill's crest, suspecting what the murmurs of voices were saying.

They could have everything their cold, weary, aching, embittered hearts longed for, thought Alaren, *if only they were willing to give up this war.*

He settled his peaked and crooked hat firmly on his head,

looked up to the breathless sparkle of stars above, and stepped out onto the crest of the hill that rose like a dragon's spine between the two freezing armies. The crunch of his footsteps over the hard snow fired like drum beats into the still night.

"Who's that?" whispered one of the sentries for Marin's army, peering at the figure slowly walking up the ridgeline, dark against the blacker ink of the moonless night.

"Alaren," his companion breathed, pointing at the crooked hat that caught the faint glimmer of starlight.

"What's he doing, for ancestors' sake?"

"Getting himself killed, like as not," the other sentry swore. "I'm going to pass word to the men to stand down before some dim-witted, near-sighted, bare-chinned boy shoots an arrow through the fool's heart."

He shook his head at the folly of their king's youngest brother. The tall fellow had been trailing the armies for weeks, trying to talk sense into his warring brothers and their warriors. An order had gone out to leave Alaren alone; no one was to harm him, no one was to help him.

Across the hill, Shirar's warriors blinked the frost out of their eyelashes. Gloved hands rose to stop their companions from taking action, heads shook as some reached for bows. The name of Alaren leapt from one to the next and the tired warriors sat back.

The lean figure on the crest of the hill pulled something out of the folds of his long cloak. He lifted it to his chin. In the clear, frigid air, the first notes of an old fiddle's lament sang out.

In the hills on either side of Alaren, faces grew stony with sorrow. The bodies of their friends lay strewn throughout these hills, buried in hasty graves, their funeral songs unsung.

"He's playing for their souls tonight, laying them to rest proper," said a warrior in a blue tunic.

"He's playing for our hearts tonight, knowing our losses," said a warrior in a red jacket.

Alaren's lament walked the hills. The sound seemed to crouch down beside each man and rest a hand upon his shoulder. Eyes grew tight with unshed tears. The youngest boys wept openly, the tears freezing on scarves and collars.

The lament ended. The last, lingering note faded away. Silence fell and the eternity of night deepened.

"Don't stop."

The voice rang out across the snow. The warriors on the opposite side jolted at the sound of their enemy's voice.

"I must, friends," Alaren said, casting his words left and right to include them all, holding up his bow and fiddle. "My fingers will freeze without a fire."

A disappointed silence fell. Then the sound of footsteps running across snow crunched loudly. The shape of a boy crested the ridge. The clunk of firewood and rustle of kindling sounded.

"Here. Please."

The grizzled old men among the boy's enemies hung their heads, recognizing the cracking voices of their young sons in the youth's pleading words. They could hear his nightmares and his fears crowding up against his throat. They could sense his longing for the end of fighting spilling into those two simple words.

"Does anyone have a flint stone?" Alaren called quietly down to the warriors.

"Aye," a gruff voice replied.

The sound of his slow, weighted steps climbed the side of the hill. A spark flared against the night. Another. A crackle erupted. A blaze grew.

Light.

Two hundred longing eyes leapt to the hope of that fire, shining like a candle under the unbearable black cold of the longest night of the year. Alaren stood alone. The boy and man had backed warily away as the light illuminated their faces. Alaren played a second song, an old tune, known to all of them. At the third refrain, a second fiddle joined his from the encampment to his left. By the fifth verse, a voice on his right rose upon the night air, cracked and strong at the same time.

Alaren bowed the tune into another, gliding seamlessly from one song to the next. A dozen voices picked up the verses. It was as if the hills on one side of Alaren sang out to the other.

Midway through, the first singer stepped out of hiding and walked up the hill toward the fire. He came without weapons and held his hands out as he sang to show he would do no harm that night. His comrades watched him breathlessly, certain he would be struck down in the next heartbeat.

Then another face popped over the ridge, a lad, singing, carrying nothing more than another log of firewood, which he fed to the blaze.

Alaren's eyes stung with emotion as the two singers' eyes met and the fear of the enemy gave way to the recognition of their shared humanity. As he licked the salt off his lips, another warrior joined them, holding out his weaponless hands to the warmth of the fire. The next man brought a loaf of bread and broke it with the next youth who crept out of the darkness.

Alaren played until his bowstrings frayed and his fiddle shuddered out of tune in the cold. He played until his arms ached and his eyes dropped with weariness. He played every song he knew twice over, and when he faltered, another man stepped up. This bearded man took the fiddle from Alaren's cold fingers and tuned it true, lifting the body under his beard and playing the songs of his homeland.

The truce lasted three days and three nights, and we now call these the Feast Days of the Three Brothers . . . one for Marin, one for Shirar, and the third night for the peace of Alaren. No fighting. No warring. No attacks happened during this time.

On the fourth day, the commanders rode through the ranks of their mutinying men and threatened to hang any traitor who refused to fight. Despite this, the war ended a month later. And, while the history books give other reasons to explain the end of the war, the truth is that Alaren won peace on the longest night of the year by inviting them all to join him. People who sing and break bread around the fire together can no longer fight as enemies. Instead, they strive for peace together as friends.

~ The End ~

Behind the Story - Real Life Inspiration
Christmas Truce

This story is inspired by the true story of the Christmas Truce during World War I where nearly 100,000 French, British, and German soldiers participated in an unofficial ceasefire around the Christmas holidays of 1914. The ceasefire started in bits and pieces. In the week leading up to Christmas, British, French, and German soldiers trekked across the trenches to exchange holiday greetings. Soldiers from both sides ventured into no man's land on Christmas Eve and Christmas Day to celebrate and give each other food and gifts. Joint burial ceremonies and prisoner swaps took place. Some reports say that a few meetings concluded with carol singing. The enemies who - just days before - had been massacring each other in brutal trench warfare were now setting aside weapons to play sports together.

After the holidays, the war resumed. The following year, the commanders issued strongly worded orders to keep the soldiers from joining into another unofficial ceasefire, fearing that it would undermine the willingness to keep fighting.

Alaren's fictional story also draws from the folktale, Stone Soup, in which bitterly divided townspeople realize that they have enough to take care of each other, if only they will share their resources as a whole. As each person brings their single carrot, potato, or herb, they find that they are able to make a wonderful meal for everyone. Alaren's tale includes this in the way the soldiers bring firewood and matches, fiddles and bread.

Discussion Questions:

- When people are tired of fighting, what are some things that can help them stop?
- How do we end war when we know we no longer want to fight?
- This story says, "They could have everything their cold, weary, aching, embittered hearts longed for, thought Alaren, if only they were willing to give up this war." If this is true, then why did the men and boys not give up the war, despite their suffering?

- The Grandmothers Sit-In to Stop the War -
To stand up for peace, they had to sit down against war.

At last, the day came when everyone (except Marin and Shirar) was sick of war. Even the warriors were tired of fighting. Finally, peace negotiations were arranged to take place in the village encircled by the Brothers Walls. A barn was used as a meeting hall. The two kings were housed in the two finest homes. The armies camped on either side of the village. Everyone held their breaths and waited.

Alaren had been barred from the talks for the simple reason that each of his brothers accused him of being in league with the other brother. Any suggestion he put forth, no matter how fair or compromising, was automatically rejected by Marin and Shirar. So, Alaren stayed out-of-sight, but close by where he could follow any signs of progress - or lack thereof. He had worked hard to initiate these peace talks, but rumor had it that the conversations were not going well. In fact, it sounded like wind rattling the leaves on the trees: all bluster and no substance.

"They'll never reach peace," everyone moaned.

With the armies of Marin and Shirar camped on opposite sides of the village, Alaren's Peace Force had their hands full de-escalating tensions and arguments between the two. Fortunately, everyone was so exhausted that they mostly stayed in their tents, fixed their gear, and prayed the two kings would come to some agreement so everyone could go home.

"It isn't working," the chief steward (in charge of drinks and refreshments) groaned, exiting the barn and shaking his head as Alaren pressed him for details.

"They don't even try," the steward complained. "They're just posturing, bluffing, bragging, and threatening each other day after day. They're stalling, no doubt, wasting time until they can each storm out of here claiming that he tried to make peace but the other brother refused to meet him halfway."

Alaren sighed.

"When we were little, they tried that on my mother and she sat in front of their room refusing to let them out for supper until they made peace."

"May she rest with the ancestors," the steward said reverently. Then he added, "I take that back - I wish she'd come back from the dead to haunt them . . . or at least sit outside that barn door until they made peace!"

Alaren chuckled. Then he had an idea.

The following morning, after Marin and Shirar entered the barn, a group of old women from the Border Mountain villages, members of Alaren's Peace Force, came and sat down outside the front door. They waited quietly for hours as the armies watched curiously. Then, just before noon, Marin hurtled out of the barn, shouting something about an imbecilic brother who wouldn't see reason -

Marin broke off and skidded to an abrupt halt. A wall of women faced him, shoulder-to-shoulder, cutting off his path. He skirted to the left; they blocked him. He dodged right; they stood in his way.

"Go back in there and make peace with your brother," said the oldest grandmother sternly.

Marin reached for his sword only to remember that he'd put it aside according to the conditions of the peace talks. He whirled and went back in. A couple moments later, Shirar came roaring out, calling for his army.

"If you ever want to see an end to war," one of the women called out to the soldiers, "you'll stay right where you are."

They stayed put.

By nightfall, women were coming from all directions to join the original group. Hundreds, then thousands, made the journey to hold Marin and Shirar to the task of reaching peace. When a treaty was signed and stamped, the two kings came out the door of the barn and held it aloft for all to see.

"There," they roared in one voice, "we've made peace. Now let us through."

The women laughed and cheered and opened a pathway to let the kings - and the peace they'd made - come out into the world.

~ The End ~

Behind the Story - Real Life Inspiration
Women of Liberia Mass Action for Peace

This story is inspired by the true story of the Women of Liberia Mass Action for Peace that stopped the second Liberian Civil War in 2001 and ousted the dictator Charles Taylor. The women managed to secure peace talks between Charles Taylor and the various rebel factions, but the men were stalling and boasting, threatening and refusing to make peace. So, the women sat down in front of the doors of the negotiations hall and refused to leave until the treaty was signed. It worked!

The women used many tactics in the lead-up to this moment. They had held mass demonstrations for months and used peacebuilding to connect to the many factions of the war. After the peace talks, they organized a weapons buy-back program. Charles Taylor resigned and, in 2006, one of the main organizers of the Women of Liberia Mass Action for Peace, Ellen Johnson Sirleaf, was elected as the first female president of Liberia.

You can learn more about the Women of Liberia Mass Action for Peace in the amazing documentary film, *Pray the Devil Back To Hell*.

Alaren's tale draws on the use of people-power to hold leaders to their promises of making peace. The grandmothers block the doors of the barn until the kings sign a treaty. The warriors assist them by refusing to obey Shirar's order to move the women. Other people - elders, children, women - come to help them maintain the blockade. When we work for peace, everyone has a role to play.

Discussion Questions:

- What would you be willing to do for peace?
- Would you sit down in front of the doors and refuse to leave until peace was reached?
- Why is it important that the soldiers are willing to stand back and not intervene?

- Waging Peace -

When the war ended, Alaren felt his work had only just begun. Peace was a practice, not a declaration made by kings. In order for peace to last, everyone had to be part of the effort to heal from the war. They had to grieve and mourn, tell true stories and repair broken relationships. They had to strengthen their communities and develop different ways to deal with conflict. Alaren believed that unless people actively tried to heal, the scars of war would always fester and bleed. Those wounds, if left unchecked, would cause the next war. Here are some of the many ways Alaren and his friends worked to heal from the war and wage peace.

- A Hundred Ways of Healing -
Alaren faced the most difficult task of his life.

The Brothers War had ended, but innumerable festering wounds of anger, resentment, bitterness, fear, loss, and hatred lingered among all of the people. Even the brightest summer days were clouded by the pains of the past. Alaren and his Peace Force thought their work would be done when the war ended. Instead, they found it had only just begun. Again and again, the followers of the Way Between interrupted fights and de-escalated hostilities and stopped the vicious cycle of blood feuds.

"Alaren," they would say to him, exhausted after another day of keeping conflicts from igniting back into violence and war, "the stories people tell . . . they need to be heard . . . by each other, not just by us."

Marin's farmers needed to hear why the Shirar's shepherds got into fistfights over little slights. Shirar's traders needed to understand why Marin's housewives locked their doors and set the dogs on them. Truths needed to be heard. Wounds needed to be healed. Apologies needed to be issued. Forgiveness needed to be spoken. Reconciliations needed to be supported.

So, Alaren began the most difficult task of his life: gathering people to speak the unspeakable, to say what had happened, to show the broken pieces of their hearts, to express their fears and hatreds, and to hear the other side of all the stories.

His Peace Force formed a council. Their job was to listen, record, and keep fights from breaking out as people spoke one by one. They went to sites of massacres and atrocities and terrible battles and let the true stories be spoken. They sat down with widows and orphans and made space for warriors to hear their sorrows. They brought together veterans to hear veterans from opposite sides of the war speak.

Slowly, after years of listening, the bottled-up pain in everyone's hearts began to release and shift. Alaren set up reconciliation teams to deal with the seething resentments and gaping wounds left over from the war. They held restorative justice circles that worked tirelessly to heal traumas and address wrongs. They created processes for holding armies and soldiers accountable when the Kings Marin and Shirar chose to overlook the harm done by their armies. The Peace Force held truth-speakings in which members of the Peace Force role-played the parts of warriors' spirits so the survivors could speak with the dead and find closure.

Alaren's Peace Force invented a hundred ways of healing. They never stopped this work. Generations bore the scars of war. Every act of violence left its mark on the children of the children of the ones involved in the violence. Alaren sometimes felt creating peace was harder than trying to turn a river upstream, but whenever he said this, someone would disagree, reminding him that war was the river turned backwards. Peace was as natural as a laughing stream, flowing down into the earth and making the green things grow.

~ The End ~

Behind the Story - Real Life Inspiration
Truth and Reconciliation Commissions

Many people have heard of the South African Truth and Reconciliation Commission after the end of apartheid. But did you know that hundreds of such hearings have been held all over the world? The Museum of Memory and Human Rights in Santiago, Chile, displays a global map of photos representing all the places in the world that have used truth and reconciliation commissions.

A truth commission:

- is focused on the past, rather than ongoing events;
- investigates a pattern of events that took place over a period of time;
- engages directly and broadly with the affected population, gathering information on their experiences;
- is a temporary body, with the aim of concluding with a final report;
- and, is officially authorized or empowered by the state under review.

Truth and Reconciliation Commissions have been used in several South and Central American countries (Chile, Argentina, Bolivia, Guatemala) in the wake of brutal military regimes. In Canada, Australia, and in certain parts of the United States, Truth and Reconciliation Commissions are being used to address the painful history of residential schools and the theft of Native children from their parents, tribes, and nations. In Rwanda, a commission deals with the aftermath of the Rwandan genocide. In Liberia and Sierra Leone, the Truth and Reconciliation Commissions focus on civil wars.

The stories continue. The Wikipedia page on Truth and

Reconciliation includes a list of all the places where these commissions have been held. They can be a powerful part of societal healing and effective tools for accountability, truth-telling, and humanizing the effects of violence.

Discussion Questions:

- Where else could a Truth and Reconciliation Commission be used in our world today?
- How could a Truth and Reconciliation Commission help your local community?

- Remembering Who You Are -
He had killed. Could he ever be anything but a killer?

Alaren stepped cautiously through the mist. Dawn's thick fog cloaked the foothills. Out there, hidden in the gray, the war's cast-off youths either slept like logs or aimed their arrows at his heart. After the peace treaty between Marin and Shirar, many of the young soldiers had returned home, but packs of them, alienated from villages that had supported the opposite army, still roamed the Border Mountains. They raided villages, plundered caravans, and battled with each other. Alaren had come to put a stop to that.

He paused. His ears tensed, listening. He took a step to the left. Paused. Stepped again. Paused. Moved to take a third step-

- and halted with his foot in the air.

Just beneath him, a boy - for he was only that, not quite a man despite the horrors he'd seen and done - lay curled on his side, sound asleep. One hand clenched his bow; the other squeezed an arrow. Alaren lowered his foot back to the ground. He pulled his gray cloak tighter about his thin shoulders and crouched down on his heels to wait. He pulled the hood over his head and sat so still a bird landed on his shoulder, thinking he was just one of the mid-sized boulders strewn about the area.

The bird warbled. The sun parted the fog. The boy groaned and opened his eyes.

"Good morning," Alaren said softly.

The boy leapt up with a wild shout, dropping his arrow and flailing for the quiver on his back.

"I mean you no harm," Alaren told him quickly. "I am Alaren."

The youth froze, recognizing the name. His eyes ran over the lanky limbs of the calm, silver-haired man.

"What do you want?" he asked harshly, his voice cracked as a crow's caw, exhausted with bitterness.

"Your mother asked me to find you," Alaren said, an aching compassion in his voice.

The boy shuddered. A flicker of yearning glowed in his eyes, but he shook his head.

"I can't. They'll hate me."

Alaren had heard these words a hundred times before from other youths like this, frightened and filthy, hiding in the hills and stealing from villagers.

"Why would they hate you?" Alaren asked. He knew the answer, but speaking truth would help the boy.

"I've done things," the youth said gruffly. "Horrible things."

He choked up and hid his face. It wasn't the battles that tormented him - though he'd been scared witless every time, slashing his sword and just hoping to survive. No, the battles were cruel and terrifying, but they did not wring his soul in knots. It was the later deaths that haunted him, the ones from the bandit raids: the girl's screams in the burning hut, the old man clutching his chest and toppling over, the child thrown against a stone wall with a sickening crack to the skull. He had nightmares about the way he'd found himself standing over his cousin as the youth died from his sword thrust.

"I - I can't go back," the youth stuttered. "My mother - I'm better off dead to her."

"That's not what she thinks," Alaren answered.

"She doesn't know what I've done."

Alaren cleared his throat and stared stonily at the boy.

"She lived through the war. She has an idea, no doubt."

The youth shrugged.

"There's nothing for me now but this life," he replied.

"Nonsense," Alaren objected. "The people in your village talk about you all the time."

"What do they say? That I'm a traitor? A coward? A murderer?" the boy asked bitterly.

"Some," Alaren told him honestly, "but more talk about how you were always a bright boy. You had strong convictions and passions. That you cared about people and wanted to protect them."

The youth's eyes turned red around the rims.

"Come back with me," Alaren coaxed. "Hear what they have to say, for better or for worse, and carve out a new life that doesn't involve stealing and attacking the villages. You are better than this."

Alaren talked from dawn until noon, growing hoarse and thirsty and hungry. He paused to break bread with the youth, who scarfed down his half of the loaf in four gulping bites.

"Your grandmother made that," Alaren mentioned. "She has another loaf at home, waiting for you if you come hear what she has to say."

A wild look of fear touched the boy's eyes.

"You owe it to them to at least listen," Alaren told him firmly, rising, "then you can disappear from their lives and live like a bandit."

It took until late afternoon, but the boy finally agreed to come with Alaren back to his old village. They went to his mother's house first. She was stirring a pot of soup when he came in and, though he thought she might yell or cry, she did neither.

"Listen to me," she said, "I want to remind you of who you are."

She spoke of the son who gave smiles to everyone and a helping hand to whoever needed it. She told him how much he reminded her of his father, proud and strong - perhaps headstrong, she admitted. She reminded him of his skills at carpentry and pointed to the roof beams he had helped to replace before the war.

"I am a murderer," he answered in a small voice.

She shook her head.

"You have murdered, yes, but that is not who you are. It was not who you were, and it is not who you will be for your whole life. Go listen to your grandmother if you do not believe me."

Alaren walked with the youth to the old woman's house.

"Do you remember," she told her grandson, "when you broke our ancestors' clay jar? How you came to me with the pieces in your hands and told me you couldn't put it back together? You asked me to forgive you and I did."

Tears ran down the youth's face as he nodded.

"That is who you are. You have done things that cannot be fixed, cannot ever be repaired to how they were before . . . but you are strong enough to apologize and humble enough to ask for forgiveness. That is who you are. Go and speak to your aunt."

The youth swallowed hard. This was the mother of the cousin he had killed. His knees shook, but he took his grandmother's words to heart and followed Alaren to the next house. He was shocked by what he saw. His aunt had been a proud woman, proud of her son and her finely-kept house, proud of her abundant garden and soft wool, proud of the architecture and carpentry of her husband. But now, everything had fallen into ruin. The garden wilted and withered. The blankets hung gray and worn on the clothesline. The fences tilted. The roof sagged and one corner had caved in. Inside, his aunt slumped in a chair, her hair unkempt and her face lined with bitter grief at having lost her husband and son.

"Aunt . . ." he began, and then could say nothing more.

Without a word, he took the heavy bucket of well water up and refilled the kettle. He went out into the yard, split her wood, and stoked up the ashes of her fire. He brought fresh vegetables and made her a soup, washed the dishes piled up in a bucket, and aired out the back-bedroom's must and mold. She stared at him with silent eyes. Alaren watched them both quietly. As dusk deepened into darkness, the aunt fell asleep by the fire and the youth put a blanket over her knees.

"Who are you?" Alaren asked him suddenly. "Do you remember now?"

The boy slowly nodded.

"I am someone who has done wrong, broken things that cannot be fixed, but I am also someone who knows how to care for people."

"And tomorrow, who will you be? Bandit or villager? Where will you put the rest of your life's breath?"

The youth looked around. There was work to be done here. It would be hard. It would be a long time before he could confess to his aunt what he had done, who it really was who had killed her son. It would be ages until he felt he could meet his family's eyes again. But he also knew where his heart told him he should be.

"I will stay," he answered Alaren.

The thin man rose and smiled. He squeezed the youth's shoulder and left. The darkness had settled on the foothills and he had a long moonlit walk ahead of him. Alaren headed to the places where the youths hid, waiting for someone to call them home.

~ The End ~

Behind the Story - Real Life Inspiration
Indigenous Practices for Reconnecting with Youth

This story is based in part on a story I heard about the restorative practices of some of the Northwest Native tribes. In one of them, when a youth started to lose their way, adults and elders would seek out the young person (often seemingly at random) and spend some time with them. Perhaps they would go fishing. Or the elder would ask for help with a task. Or they'd walk for a short way together. While they did this, the adult or elder would speak about the youth, recalling the beautiful things about this young person. They would bring up strong, positive qualities the youth embodied. They would retell stories of the good things the young person had done. They'd remark on the kind or generous actions the person might have recently taken. Slowly but surely, they'd remind the person of who they really are, breaking the cycle of negative stories, and opening a pathway toward healing and repairing any harm that might have been done.

Discussion Questions:

- Have you ever done something that you regretted? Were you forgiven? If not, why not. If so, how did you mend the relationship?
- What does forgiveness feel like, whether you've forgiven someone, or you have been forgiven?

- Breathing Fire: From Throwing Stones
to Holding Dialogues -
Could the kids and soldiers ever stop harassing each other
to the brink of war?

"If those kids throw one more stone, they'll set the whole war off again!" the captain shouted in frustration.

Alaren rubbed his temples. If the man's soldiers would quit breathing down the kids' necks, they wouldn't be chucking pebbles in irritation at the army!

He thought it prudent to hold his tongue until he thought of a more tactful way to explain this to the captain. The fellow argued that he was simply keeping troublemakers in line. After all, he informed Alaren, the army had a duty to shake down the villagers every few days and confiscate all weapons in order to keep the tenuous peace.

The fact that the villagers only kept weapons because they were afraid of the army camped at their gate seemed to escape the captain's comprehension. Everywhere the hard, stern man put his foot down, irritation and resentment broke out. The soldiers were supposed to uphold the laws, protect the villagers, and make sure any criminals were brought before the magistrate.

Thus far, Alaren had been unimpressed. The soldiers broke up fights by beating everyone in reach. They stopped thieves by flinging daggers in their backs. They hauled the village boys up before the magistrate for crimes like "looking surly" and "hanging about".

The youths weren't saints, Alaren admitted with a snort, but they were human, adolescents at that, lacking judgment and notoriously immature.

Take stones, for example. Nothing amused the boys more than flinging a tiny pebble - no bigger than a dried pea - at a soldier and seeing him slap the sting as if it were a fly bite. The boys' giggles would give them away, and the soldiers' reactions to the prank had largely involved throwing something heavier or sharper back at the boys.

All it would take was one dead boy to set the tinderbox of resentments off into a blazing wildfire of violence.

Something had to be done . . . and Alaren had an idea.

When he first suggested the notion to the captain, however, the answer was a resounding: No. Never. Not even if you paid me.

Then the soldiers hauled a pack of village boys before the magistrate calling for their heads on a platter or their tails behind bars for the rest of their days. They were accused of siphoning off a batch of the soldiers' home-brewed whiskey and selling it back to them after their distilling efforts had mysteriously evaporated. Alaren tried not to laugh - the situation was quite serious - but if any of those soldiers had been innocent of similar antics at that age, he'd eat his walking stick. The boys had, apparently, sampled their wares and gotten a bit carried away. They'd managed to light sprays of alcohol on fire, pretending to be fire-breathing dragons - or a certain red-faced, irate army captain - and they had been caught when they accidentally set one of the army tents on fire.

The magistrate had dealt with three of the seven boys twice

this month already. He looked ready to lock them in a root cellar simply to get some peace and quiet. The boys' mothers were distraught, convinced their sons were about to hang. A brawl between protective older brothers and soldiers seemed imminent. Alaren stepped up to the magistrate and whispered his idea in the man's ear. Bushy white eyebrows drew down into a scowl of thought.

"If they all kill each other, this is on your head," he warned Alaren.

Then he sentenced the boys to ten meetings with Alaren and the irate soldiers.

No one thought it would work. Everyone predicted disaster. Bets were placed on who would wind up with the first black eye: the soldiers, the boys, or Alaren? But, after ten meetings, something shifted. The boys stopped throwing stones and pulling pranks. The soldiers quit arresting them for minor reasons. The entire town breathed a sigh of relief.

"What did you do?" people asked Alaren, imagining the soldiers must have used dire threats to terrify the boys.

"We told stories," Alaren answered with a shrug.

True stories, painful stories, hard stories. The soldiers spoke about being the boys' age, once. The boys spoke about what they hoped to do when they were as old as the soldiers. They swapped honest impressions of each other - a long list of nasty insults that made everyone mad until Alaren encouraged them all to explain what they meant.

"He's an uptight warthog because he won't let us do anything fun!" a youth complained about a certain soldier.

"They're immature lay-abouts who have no appreciation for the difficulty of our job!" a soldier hollered back.

"Your job is to annoy us," another boy grumbled.

"Oh? I thought that was your job description, not ours," a

soldier shot back at the boy.

"Didn't you ever do stuff like this when you were our age?" a lad grumbled.

Suddenly, a glimmer of understanding opened up. The soldiers' eyes filled with memories. As the meeting went on, the youths explained why they threw stones. The soldiers explained why it annoyed them so much. Groans of sudden realizations rippled through the room. Exasperated sighs gave rise to pragmatic solutions. Grumbles shifted into good-humored banter. A few chuckles broke out. Finally, the two groups understood who the other was and how to live in the same small village together.

In the last of the ten sessions, one of the soldiers put up his hand.

"Now, there's something I need from all of you boys," he began.

A round of groans lifted. They'd already made a half dozen promises to quit throwing stones and stealing whiskey and annoying the soldiers. What more could the soldier want?

"I can't leave," the man said, pulling out a match and a flask, "without learning how to breathe fire."

~ The End ~

Behind the Story - Real Life Inspiration
Police-Youth Dialogues in Gainesville, Florida

This story is based on the Police-Youth Dialogues in Gainesville, Florida, organized and facilitated by the River

Phoenix Center for Peacebuilding (RPCP). In 2012, the Chief of the Gainesville Police Department contacted RPCP for assistance as they recognized that Gainesville had a juvenile justice problem. A disproportionate number of African American youth were being suspended and arrested at a higher rate than white youth. Police officers often escalated interactions with youth on the street and in schools and most of these did not need to result in arrests.

The River Phoenix Center for Peacebuilding had introduced restorative justice in the schools previously, but they quickly realized that the youth and police held deep-seated grievances and mistrust of one another. These grievances were fueling negative cycles of arrest and incarceration, so RPCP partnered with law enforcement and hosted their first series of Police-Youth Dialogues.

They describe the program as "a bold and innovative approach to facilitate healing and trust by bringing together black and brown youth and Law Enforcement Officers to address issues and concerns that impact their daily lives. Through direct dialogue and dynamic interactions, we are dismantling layers of prejudice, stereotypes, bias, fear and mistrust between these groups and finding common ground. This is an important first step in a long and winding path of rebuilding trust."

In each Police-Youth Dialogue series, a wide variety of youth and police officers come together to participate in a set of exercises, games, role play, food and conversations that reveal hard truths. All of these help the two groups see each other with new eyes. Police learn how youth often react from unmet needs and past trauma. They also gain a better understanding of the adolescent brain, de-escalation skills, and how to help youth connect with resources in their community to help meet their needs. Rather than arresting the youth for "attitude problems", police officers learn ways to support youth in transforming the conflicts they face. Likewise, youth learn to see officers as human beings who can live up to their motto of "protect and serve." The program has now conducted over 100 trainings and served over 3,000 participants.

Discussion Questions:

- Is there a need for skillfully facilitated dialogues (like the ones in this story and in Gainesville, Florida) in your community? Who would need to be involved? What would one goal be for this type of restorative work?
- If you were invited to participate in a dialogue like this, would you be involved? Who might the two groups be?

- Gather Berries, Share Peace -
The villagers had the right to hunt, fish, and gather
. . . but they were too afraid of the soldiers to try.

"In the peace treaty," Alaren explained for the third time, "it was agreed that the stream belongs to Shirar, but the village retains the right to hunt, fish, and gather on both banks."

The villagers shook their heads at the stork-like man. They pointed to the army outpost on the other side of the stream and told him that the soldiers would kill them if they got too close.

"Have you tried?" Alaren sighed.

Heads shook. No one was foolish enough to try the patience of Shirar's soldiers. The Brothers War between Marin and Shirar had ended nearly a year ago, but every village boy or girl still hauled water from the well a mile away instead of from the nearby river.

Alaren chewed his lower lip. During the tense peace negotiations with Shirar and Marin, he had spent countless hours trying to make sure that the villagers in the Border Mountains would be able to gather food and water like they always had. Cutting off the villages' food and water supply was a recipe for seething resentments and eventual attacks from desperate and starving people. If the villages attacked the soldiers, the Border Mountains would be aflame with war again.

"I'll talk with Shirar's soldiers," Alaren told the villagers, removing his boots and rolling up his cuffs as he waded through a shallow ford to the other side of the river.

He lifted his famous white flag with its Mark of Peace. Resting the pole end against his hip, he plucked a handful of wild berries from the tangled thorns at the river's edge.

"Alaren," the sentry stated, both cautious and curious.

"Care for a berry?" he offered.

"Sure," the sentry answered. He'd been eyeing the brambles all day hoping to pick a few when his shift was done.

"Is your captain around?" Alaren asked.

"Yes, sir. He's right in that tent there."

Alaren nodded and made his way over, handing out berries to every soldier along the way.

"Alaren, what brings you over to this side of the river?" the captain asked, cordially rising to greet his king's younger brother.

"The berries are ripe," he offered, holding out his hand.

The captain accepted and gestured for Alaren to pull up a chair.

"What are you really here for?" he asked.

"Peace, of course," Alaren answered with a smile. "The villagers wish to hold a feast and invite you and a few men . . . you know, break bread instead of necks, that sort of thing."

The captain scowled skeptically for a moment then shrugged. What could it hurt? He agreed to join the villagers so long as Alaren and his followers of the Way Between were present to ensure it was not an ambush.

Alaren smiled and picked up his flag.

"I will see you tomorrow night, then," he told the captain. "Only, the villagers will need to fish and gather berries along the river. I trust you will tell your men?"

"Yes, yes, that's fine," the captain said brusquely, waving at

Alaren to take his leave.

Alaren had a more difficult time convincing the villagers.

"A feast?" the mother of the headman cried. "Dinner and dessert and all that? You want us to cook pies for those brutes?"

Alaren thanked the ancestors that he'd convinced his brothers to rotate the troops after the end of the war - the villagers would have flat-out refused to cook for the murderers of their sons and husbands. As it was, they still objected loudly to cooking for these strangers in the uniforms of their enemies.

"One meal in trade for a lifetime of meals for your children," Alaren coaxed persuasively, "is worth swallowing anger and pride, and making friends out of former enemies."

When the headman's ancient grandmother smacked her lips and declared that she'd like one more taste of river fish before she died, Alaren knew he'd won.

Cautiously, the villagers made their way down to the riverbanks, eyeing the soldiers warily. A guard nodded. A child waved. The morning proceeded without incident. The aromas of roasting fish and baking pies rose on the breeze and when the time of the feast arrived, the soldiers who were not selected to attend looked wistfully across the river.

"If you let the villagers fish and gather on a regular basis," Alaren told them, "I'd imagine a pie or two would come your way from time to time."

On the villagers' side, he slipped a word to the headman's wife that the soldiers were praising her cooking just from the scent. If a pie or two made it across the river, he'd bet the soldiers would have no objections to the villagers regularly gathering and fishing along the riverbanks.

Three pies slipped across the ford that night, followed by many more in the weeks to come. Each day, the villagers approached the river. Each day, the soldiers did not stop them.

Day after day, the peace treaty's rights were upheld. And some days, the soldiers even helped gather berries for the pies.

Alaren popped a berry into his mouth and smiled.

~ The End ~

Behind the Story - Real Life Inspiration
The Anishinabe Treaty Rights Struggle

This story draws loosely from the Anishinabe (also called Ojibwe or Chippewa) Treaty Rights struggle of Native people in Wisconsin, Michigan, and Minnesota. They had researched the treaties between their nations and the United States and discovered that their forbearers had reserved the right to hunt, fish, and gather on large swathes of land and water (rivers and lakes) ceded to the United States. In the 1980s, they started to assert those rights using nonviolent means.

In Northern Wisconsin, the Ojibwe would go to the shore of Butternut Lake to go spearfishing (a traditional way of fishing that uses a torch at the end of a canoe at night to attract the fish and a spear to catch them). Crowds of angry non-Native locals gathered to harass and threaten them, but they persevered. For three years, these scenes repeated. In the end, through steadfast nonviolent action, drawing on what they called the "Anishinabe way", the Ojibwe succeeded in shifting the views of the communities surrounding them, flipping the non-Natives' attitudes from virulent hostility to understanding and support.

In my fictional story, the villagers retain the right to gather and fish after the end of the war, but antagonism and the presence of armed soldiers keep the villagers from exercising those rights. Alaren suggests a campaign of nonviolent action, designed to disarm the hostility of the soldiers and asserted their rights through exercising them.

Discussion Questions:

- What are your rights? (Civil, human, legal, etc.)
- Do you have any rights you're not using? What would happen if you - and everyone else - exercised them?
- How can sharing food help build peace and community?

- Alaren and the Shoes -

How could he remind Marin of the true cost of war?

Alaren strode down the street, angry and worried. Marin was visiting this mid-sized city in the eastern foothills and he had come to pull his brother back from starting another war.

"Have you already forgotten the sons and daughters killed in your last war?!" he had just shouted at his brother, moments before he stormed out the door.

Alaren winced. He rarely lost his temper - it didn't seem to do much good when he did - but Marin was planning to make war on their brother Shirar again. He was preparing to attack this summer over nothing more than the insults Shirar had sent in his last letter.

"He's been calling you an idiot since he was six," Alaren had pointed out as Marin had swept everything off the table in a fit of rage.

"Yes, well, I pounded him then and I'll do it again!" Marin swore.

"If you want to get into a fistfight with your brother, that's one thing - a terrible thing - but don't go dragging other people into a war," Alaren begged.

But that was exactly what Marin raged about doing . . . again. Alaren rubbed his face with his palm and felt the dampness of tears. Just yesterday, he had comforted a friend of his, a widow who had lost her husband and son in the last war, as she wept over a pair of her son's baby shoes.

Marin should see that mother's tears, Alaren thought grimly. Marin should see the rows of shoes by the door that the widows dusted in their housekeeping rounds, unable to get rid of the hope that, one day, their loved ones would return and fill those shoes.

Alaren skidded to a halt in the street.

Those shoes, he thought, *are precisely what Marin should see.*

He turned around, crossed the city, and knocked on the door of his widowed friend.

"I need to borrow your shoes," he said gently.

Two days later, the river mist lifted upon a strange sight . . . the street outside Marin's lodgings was filled with shoes, large and small, women's, men's, children's, dancing heels and sturdy work boots: shoes whose occupants would never again dance, stride, pace, or climb in them.

When Marin came to the gate, he saw thousands of empty shoes paired and pointing at him like an army of ghosts. Behind them, lining the edges of the street, stood the mothers, fathers, sisters, wives, and others who had brought their loved ones' shoes. Young widows held their fatherless babes. Masters of trades carried the tools of lost apprentices in their hands, reminders of the long-term costs of war. Old people tottered up, clutching each other's arms; their wrinkled faces begged to know who would care for them in their old age.

"We don't want war," Alaren said, staring at his brother until Marin dropped his eyes, ashamed. "Promise them. Look into the eyes of your people and promise them that you will not sacrifice their loved ones to your quarrel with Shirar."

Marin promised.

By Alaren's reckoning, thousands of lives were saved by

preventing that needless war. The people picked up their loved ones' shoes and took them home. Tears were shed. Candles were lit on altars. Grief and mourning took the time they needed. But eventually, the turn of the year healed wounded hearts. New babies were given old booties. Growing youths stepped into old apprentices' work boots. New lovers met with tapping shoes and dancing heels. No one could ever replace the lost ones, but together, people eased their sorrows and carried life forward step by step.

~ The End ~

Behind the Story - Real Life Inspiration
Creative Protest

Alaren and the Shoes is based on several stories of creative action to stop war and violence that have used shoes as a silent protest. A demonstration in Washington, DC, against gun violence and mass shootings brought 7,000 pairs of children's shoes to lay upon the grass outside the Capitol Building to memorialize every child killed by gun violence since the Sandy Hook Massacre in 2012.

On the banks of the Danube River in Budapest, Hungary, a statue of shoes serves as an eternal reminder of the massacre of Hungarian Jews during WWII. The people were told to remove their shoes as they stood in a line on the riverbank. Then they were shot, their bodies falling into the river.

Other demonstrations have used a variety of personal objects to represent lives lost. An effort organized by Voices for

Creative Nonviolence called "34 Backpacks" commemorates the deaths of Yemeni children killed in an attack on August 9th, 2018. Peace activists place the backpacks in public spaces or on the steps of government buildings in a haunting reminder of the price of war.

These kinds of protests are powerful and evocative. They have been used over and over again to make a strong point.

Discussion Questions:

- What other variations of this kind of protest can you think of?
- How could you use a symbolic object like backpacks or shoes to protest an issue you care about?

- The Children's March -

How the smallest people took the biggest step for peace!

Peace had lasted long enough for infants born in the final days of war to grow up in the sunlight of happier times. But war thundered on the horizon. Marin and Shirar gathered their armies once again. Worried parents walked about with tight lips and short tempers, snapping at noisy children.

"We have to stop this war," they moaned.

Eyes turned to Alaren and his followers of the Way Between. They'd stalled and stopped so many threats of war, people had lost count. Alaren, however, was worried. Both of his brothers had warned him not to interfere upon pain of punishment of his entire Peace Force. He would have to convince the people of both nations to act for themselves.

"Come play with us!" a child called, tossing a ball in his direction.

Alaren was beloved by children throughout the lands, often stopping on his journeys to share a game, toss a ball, or tell a wild story to the young ones.

"Not today, I'm afraid," he answered ruefully. "I have to think about how to stop a war."

"War is stupid," one of the children said with a scowl, mad at losing one of their favorite full-grown playmates.

"Tell that to Marin and Shirar," Alaren sighed.

"I will," the boy boasted, puffing out his chest and poking his finger at another boy's nose, pretending his friend was one of the kings. "I'll march right up to King Marin and tell say, "War is stupid, you naughty king, stop it!"

The children collapsed in gales of laughter at the thought and quickly mimicked the boy until they'd made it into a little chant: War is stupid! Stop the war! Naughty kings, make peace!

Alaren laughed along with them . . . he wished he could tell that to his brothers.

"Would you really say that to my brothers?" he asked the children.

"If you came with us, sure," the boy answered bravely.

And that's how Alaren's Children's March began. He walked from village to village, talking to youth and parents, gathering the children at each stop until a river of small people wound through the mountains to the battlefield between Marin and Shirar. Some say that's only legend; it wasn't really a battlefield - the brothers were not that close to fighting and the Children's March had to walk hundreds of miles from one brother to the next - but whatever the truth, it worked. With thousands of children calling for peace, and all their parents trailing behind to care for them, Alaren succeeded in getting his brothers to recognize the folly of their war. Once again, peace was saved for a few more years while small children grew into youths and youths grew up, married, and had small children of their own.

~ The End ~

Behind the Story - Real Life Inspiration
Mother Jones and the Children's March

In 1903, the famous and feisty Irish-American labor organizer Mother Mary Harris Jones launched the Children's Crusade to raise awareness about the horrors of child labor. With 200 child laborers, she marched from Philadelphia, Pennsylvania, to Oyster Bay, New York, the hometown of President Theodore Roosevelt. The children carried banners that said things like, "We want to go to school and not the mines!"

The journey took several weeks with frequent stops for speeches. Many of the children had been permanently maimed by the work in the mills and mines. The exposure of these cruelties reached national attention and led to the improvement and enforcement of child labor laws in the United States.

This Alaren tale draws inspiration from the ways children can organize for social change. In our real world, we are seeing children and teens emerge as major forces in the efforts for change. In the United States, middle and high school students have been key mobilizers for ending gun violence and also stopping excessive amounts of standardized tests. Around the world, the youth are walking out of school on climate strikes, demanding an end to the climate crisis and immediate transitions to renewable energy. One of the beautiful and powerful aspects of nonviolent action is that people of all ages can use it.

Discussion Questions:

- What are some other examples of young people taking action?
- What would inspire you to take action (or to support actions taken by young people)?

- Piper's Tale -
A musician builds bridges after the war.

After the Brothers War, grief clawed peoples' hearts like a wild beast, sowing pain, fear, and in many cases, seething hatred for one's enemies. Alaren mourned deeply. A world torn asunder and soaked with blood could never return to the same place as before. Two countries now stood where once only families and neighbors had lived. Swords, arrows, armor, and colored tunics had divided peoples' hearts. They had risked their lives - and sacrificed their sons and daughters - to defend the delusions of kings. Now, when he spoke of restoring the Whole World, bitter glares and sharp words slapped him. The notion insulted the peoples' losses. To laugh at the silliness of lines and borders disrespected the fathers and cousins, husbands and sisters lying in battlefield graves.

War had accomplished what words could not. It enshrined the folly of the two nations and split the world forever.

Alaren refused to give up.

"What we need to do," he told his Peace Force, "is build a peace so strong, no war can tear it apart."

"Good luck with that," one of the shepherds from the Mariana side of the mountains sighed. "Have you heard what Shirar's people say about us? They're saying we're all-devouring dragons and throat-ripping river dogs."

"Aye," agreed a shepherd from Shirar's side of the mountains, "and the Mari Valley people claim we're demons from the desert."

Hatred festered like open sores. Fear and anger rode the winds like plague. Those, Alaren thought, were the real enemies.

"Is there anyone brave enough to go make friends with their enemy?" he asked.

Many Border Mountain villagers stepped forward, but Alaren shook his head. He needed to send Marianans to Shirar's lands and vice versa. He needed people in the shape of their enemy's fears, people who could show that those fears were unfounded.

At last, a young woman named Piper, a musician from the capital city of Mariana raised her hand.

"I'll go," she said, lifting her reed pipes, "and at least we'll have music in common, for I hear those desert demons can be transformed back into humans with a bit of sweet song."

So, Piper went down into the arid edges of the western foothills to make friends out of enemies. Her many stories could fill a whole book, but here is one every person should know.

She encountered a camp of warrior riders one evening just as dusk greyed the edges of the lowering sun. She took a deep and calming breath. The first moment of greetings were always the ones that scared her the most; that was when the sword slashed or the arrow flew, propelled by the fear of the unknown. Steadying her heart, Piper began to play a little tune to announce her arrival as she picked her way down the trail toward the glow of the warriors' campfire.

They were a fierce lot, the stuff of Piper's nightmares. Her beloved older brother had died in the war and she could easily imagine any of these bristling and rugged warriors striking the fatal blow. Her heart pounded as their heads turned in the direction of her music.

"River dog," she heard the far-seeing archer announce, shading the sunset from his eyes.

"Kill him," the leader ordered, mistaking her form for a lad's.

"Wait!" Piper cried, diving behind a boulder. "I mean no harm! I am unarmed, though I carry a rare and wonderful gift."

"And what might that be?" the leader called out suspiciously.

"Music," Piper called out simply, launching into a merry little jig she'd learned from a desert goatherd a few nights ago.

Mutters rose from the group.

"Why shouldn't we kill you, dog?" the leader hollered back.

Piper pulled the reed pipes away from her lips.

"Because if you wait until morning, you'll at least have enjoyed my music first," Piper called back cheekily.

A burst of laughter sounded.

"Alright," the leader agreed with a chuckle in his voice, "come on out. We won't kill you . . . at least not 'til morning."

"Swear on the ancestor wind!" Piper demanded, knowing that the desert dwellers didn't believe in a river of souls like her people did; they thought the spirits of their ancestors rode the wind and spoke to them in its hisses and moans.

The warriors promised - and Piper counted those vows one by one before she came to the edge of the circle playing a nervous whistle of a tune.

"What are you doing here, lass?" the warriors' leader asked.

"Well," Piper answered, "I heard a rumor that your people hated me and I wagered a bet with a friend that it wasn't true."

"You lost, fool," spat one of the men. "We'd as soon throw you to the sand lions as break bread with you."

"Yes, well, see, here's the thing," Piper stammered. "How can you hate *me* if you don't really know me?"

The warriors exchanged confused looks.

"I mean, what you really hate is war and death and those that cause it," Piper explained. "You don't really know me."

"We know you're a river dog," a warrior growled. "And that's enough."

"Ah, but there's no such thing as river dogs . . . just as you're not really desert demons," Piper countered. "If you get to know me, I wager you won't hate me."

"I'll take that wager, scum," the leader said sharply.

"Done," Piper answered promptly, "but it might take a bit of time. Until you know the answers to three questions, you don't really know who I am."

"What are the questions?" a rider asked.

"What do I fear most? What do I love best? And what do I dream of?" Piper answered, settling down on top of a low rock. She lifted the pipes and let a soft trill rise on the air. It was a desert song, one she'd learned from a band of merchants.

"You know our tunes, then?" someone asked.

Piper answered with the song. Before long, fingers tapped knees. Beards hid smiles. One man increased the soup pot by an extra portion.

"Tell me, friends," Piper asked when the song faded into the growing night. "Where do you hail from?"

"We're not your friends," the leader reminded her, but he answered the question.

Piper repaid the kindness of truth-sharing with a song from their distant hills. When she finished, throats cleared gruffly. Men surreptitiously wiped the corners of their eyes. All evening, Piper played and asked questions, listened, laughed, and cried at their stories. She spent days with the warriors, sharing tales of her own, cracking jokes, composing tunes with them, helping to cook and care for the horses.

On the seventh day, the leader pulled her aside.

"I know the answers to your questions," he said. "You love music best. You fear hatred most. And your dream is to see former enemies learning to be friends."

Piper stilled and nodded.

"And do you still hate me?" she asked quietly.

The leader sighed.

"I've tried to," he confessed, "but I cannot. You've won your wager, friend."

Piper spent the rest of her life making friends out of enemies. When the next threat of war arose, Shirar's people refused to support it, many citing their friendship with Piper and the stories she told of her people. To this day, the name for the desert people's wandering singers and storytellers is *tala* . . . which is the word for *piper* in Old Tongue. It is also, by no coincidence, the word the desert people use for friend.

~ The End ~

Behind the Story - Real Life Inspiration
Daryl Davis Builds Friendships Instead of Hate

For 30 years, Daryl Davis, a Black man, befriended Klu Klux Klan members and convinced 200 of them to leave the white supremacy group. His closet is full of robes that the former KKK members gave up. He keeps them as a reminder of the dent that he has made in racism simply by sitting down and talking to people.

Daryl would often ask a simple question, "How can you hate me if you don't even know me?"

This question and some of Daryl Davis' stories served as inspiration for this tale about Piper. He says, "When two enemies are talking, they are not fighting. It's when the talking ceases that the ground becomes fertile for violence. Keep the conversation going."

Or in Piper's case, keep the music playing.

There are folktales from around the world - both ancient and modern - about clever bards who evaded death, made friends out of enemies, and discovered how to de-escalate people's hatred. The more we know these stories, the more ideas we have for how to counter hate in our own lives.

Discussion Questions:

- In this story Piper used music as a means to get Shirar's people to truly know her. What other methods could you use to really get to know someone?
- Have you ever made friends with someone who initially disliked you? How did that happen?

- Alaren and the Bandits -
A broken leg and a sword at his throat.

Alaren was in a pickle. He stared in shocked disbelief at the odd angle of his leg. He remembered stepping out onto a deceptive scrabble of rock that flung him down the slope to the bottom of a ravine. With a loud and sickening thud-snap, his leg had broken.

He must have blacked out. The shadows crawled long behind the boulders and twisted trees. Alaren tried to stand, but the pain spun the world. He glanced at the trail above. He'd have to wait. It was a well-trodden route through the Northwest Hills. Someone would come along . . . eventually.

"Well, well, look what we have here."

Alaren groaned at the sight of the man. Of all the people! Of all the times!

The Hooded Hunter was a bandit so notorious, the village mothers threatened to call him if the children didn't behave. He was merciless and cruel, the kind of lawless raider that would shove a grandmother over a cliff in order to pull out her gold teeth. Alaren had cajoled and persuaded many robbers and bandits to return to village life, but the Hooded Hunter's band had hardened to their cruel ways. For years, the bandit leader had sent warnings to Alaren not to tangle with his men. And for years, the Hooded Hunter with his cloak and mask had kept the local soldiers hopping. Alaren had almost hoped to run into the man to see if he could persuade him to give up his raiding . . . but not when his leg was split in two.

The Hooded Hunter did not appear to recognize him. He signaled to two of his men to restrain the wounded man and search his pockets. Alaren let them. He carried little of value, anyway.

"Kill him . . . with that leg, he's good for nothing," the Hooded Hunter ordered.

"Wait!" Alaren cried. The swords were already pointing at him.

The Hooded Hunter paused.

"I can offer you something beyond measure," Alaren offered. "Something your raids and plundering cannot buy you."

He had the bandit's attention now.

"What might that be?"

"A book."

A howl of laughter met Alaren's words. The Hooded Hunter's sneer curled his lips.

"Not just any old book," Alaren clarified. "A book about you, the Hooded Hunter, and all your exploits and deeds. A book that could go in the National Library to immortalize you for all time."

Alaren told them he was a scribe - or had been before journeying to the foothills. It wasn't completely untrue; he had scribed for the archives as a youth.

"Set and bind his leg," the Hooded Hunter ordered, "and bring him along. We'll keep him . . . at least until we kill him."

And so, Alaren became the captive of the robbers, hanging tenuously between life and death at all times, scribbling away records of the band's exploits. They put the cook in charge of him and set him to peeling potatoes when they went off raiding.

In the evenings, they told a thousand tales, each one more unbelievable than the last. Alaren wrote them all down.

The bandit's life was hard, a world of danger and constant motion. Marin's soldiers had chased and ambushed them through the foothills. The bandits' ways were harsh and violent, ruled by a strict code of conduct. Alaren heard their life stories - the true ones, not just the tall tales of their exploits. Underneath the boasting were sad sagas filled with bitter losses and disappointments.

From time to time, new people showed up, begging to join the Hooded Hunter's band. Alaren wrote down their stories, too, tales of misery and poverty, hard knocks and even harder times. One man had killed a soldier in a tavern brawl. Another had escaped a gallows' noose after stealing a loaf of bread. A third had insulted the wife of a lord and been condemned to a lifetime of hard labor.

Alaren's ears burned red with shame. Many of these men came to the bandit's life because of the harsh laws passed by his brother Marin. A lad hardly old enough to attend school showed up, nearly in tears after a desperate race to escape the soldiers. He'd stolen some coins to buy medicine for his sick sister.

The bandits' way of life was not right, Alaren admitted, but neither were the laws that drove them out of their homes in the first place. The punishment for banditry was death. And so, the robbers stuck to the hills and terrorized the villages and marauded the merchants and fought with the soldiers.

Alaren had been living with the Hooded Hunter's band for half a year - spring was bursting from the trees and the weary winter had passed - when the bandit chief sat down beside him.

"How's the book?" the Hooded Hunter asked.

"Fat as the cook," Alaren answered with a smile. "Almost

ready to bring to the National Library if you will allow me to leave."

"Let me read it," the Hooded Hunter demanded.

Alaren passed him the volume and held his breath. He watched the bandit's face grow dark, his eyes mist over, his scowl deepen then unexpectedly twitch into a smile. Alaren had captured their stories, bold and true, horrid and heartbreaking. When the Hooded Hunter turned to the last page, he laid his hand on the book and sighed.

"Well, Alaren - oh yes, I learned who you were long ago - I will let you go on one condition."

"What's that?" he asked, scarcely daring to draw breath.

"You make our stories known everywhere you can."

The Hooded Hunter stared at him for a long while. If people knew what drove his men into a life of murder and robbery, perhaps they would pressure the king to change the laws.

"Remember, Alaren," the Hooded Hunter said, "if you want peace, you have to work for justice. There will never be an end to banditry if people are forced into this life because their only other option is death."

Alaren agreed to make the stories known. A short while later, as he was about to depart, the Hooded Hunter laid his hand on Alaren's shoulder.

"Thank you," he said, "for listening to our tales."

~ The End ~

Behind the Story - Real Life Inspiration
Scheherazade and the Arabian Nights

This story is one of the few Alaren tales that is not based on a true story. It is inspired by a fictional tale of nonviolent action about how a storyteller intervened and stopped a king from killing his wives.

"Alaren and the Bandits" is loosely inspired by Scheherazade, the famous fictional storyteller in *One Thousand and One Nights*. In the tale, the monarch Shahryar discovered that his first wife had been unfaithful. He killed her and resolved to marry a new wife each day, beheading the previous wife each time. To stop the murders, Scheherazade volunteered to spend one night with the king even though he planned to kill her in the morning. That night, she told him a story, but stopped in the middle, begging for an extra day of life in order to finish the tale. He agreed.

This repeated the next night, and the next, until after 1001 nights, she ran out of stories. By then, the king had fallen in love with her. He spared her life and made her his queen.

In Alaren's tale, what keeps him alive is not *his* stories, but his willingness to record the bandit's stories for posterity. Along the way, he discovers the roots of the problem leading to banditry. Storytelling and sharing our stories has been an important aspect of working for social change in numerous movements. Stories bring the injustices to life and humanize the issues for the listener. Stories help us see the problem in new ways, even help us discover solutions.

Discussion Questions:

- How can listening to someone's story help solve a problem?
- What stories could change your community if they were told and heard?
- Are you involved in a social justice or peace effort? How could storytelling be a part of that work?

- Catching the Bandits -
What is the best way to stop a bandit?

Once Alaren was released from the clutches of the Hooded Hunter, he began the long trek down from the rugged mountain cave to the swelling foothills. Spring burst from the treetops, sunny and warm. Flowers bloomed along the edges of the path. He whistled a jaunty tune - happy that his leg had healed, happy to be alive, happy to be set free. He rounded the bend with a skip in his step - and skidded to a stop.

A company of soldiers was tromping up the path. They were clanking and clunking loud enough to alert the bandits four ridgelines away. Alaren hailed them cautiously.

"Where are you headed?" he called out after introducing himself.

"We were on our way to rescue you!" the commander cried, surprised to see Alaren. "We set out as soon as the snow cleared."

"As you can see, I don't need rescuing," he replied.

"But how did you escape alive?" the commander asked.

"I wasn't a prisoner, precisely. I was more of a . . . guest while my broken leg healed."

"Well, we're still going to drive them out of the hills," the commander boasted.

Alaren had a better idea. He'd been mulling on it all winter. The bandits already had bounties on their heads. Why not put a bounty on those heads while they were still *attached* to their shoulders.

"Why not use the money to offer them land to start a village? Purchase seeds, goats, construction materials?"

"You mean, *reward* them for being bandits?" the commander exclaimed, horrified.

"No, reward them for *giving up* the bandit's life," Alaren countered. "It's safer than trying to kill them."

The commander looked unconvinced. His men liked the idea, however. Anything was better than trying to catch the Hooded Hunter and his bandits.

"They'll never surrender," the commander scoffed.

"You might be surprised," Alaren answered.

And sure enough, weeks later, the commander was surprised when Alaren appeared at the site of the experimental village with two bandits in tow. He could promise a hundred more would come down from the mountains if the first pair was alive and well at the end of the week.

By the time spring's pale green gave way to summer's golden heat, nearly a hundred former bandits had made a fresh start in the village. The soldiers were surprised at their industriousness. In no time at all, fields were planted, houses were built, and fences were set up around goat pens. The commander was stunned to see the efficient and, well, *peaceful* community emerge.

"Anyone who can uphold the bandits' code of laws can follow a new code if it offers a better chance in life," Alaren told him.

And that's how the bandits in the Northwest Hills were "caught" and offered a second chance in life.

~ The End ~

Behind the Story - Real Life Inspiration
The Dacoits and Shanti Sena

The Shanti Sena was a peace team started by M.K. Gandhi and continued by many others after his assassination. They dealt with a wide variety of issues and situations. One of these was the bandits in Chambal Valley. The dacoits (as the bandits were called) were a long-standing problem. Banditry was, for many, the only practical way of living. Kidnappings by bandits and ransom requests were commonplace. The efforts to kill the bandits by violence and force had failed. To top it all off, the on-going violence from both the bandits and the police was terrorizing the local villagers.

In 1960, Vinoba Bhave led some of his peace team members through the Chambal Valley in India, making camp and forging connections with the notorious bandits that lived in the area. Vinoba Bhave's team stopped in twenty-six villages and appealed to the dacoits to give up banditry. Twenty did so, and the peace team organized legal aid for them as well as attempted to create alternate sources of livelihood for their families. Overall, however, the effort was only a limited success. Three hundred to four hundred bandits lived in the area, and the problems continued.

But the first effort had one important impact: a decade later, when a bandit leader was considering leaving the dacoit life, the stories of Vinoba Bhave's attempt inspired him to reach out to the Shanti Sena peace team. In 1971, the bandit leader Madho Singh went in disguise to visit one of the main organizers, J.P. Narayan - a risky action, considering there was a high bounty on his head. After a long talk, the two forged a plan to get large numbers of bandits to surrender in exchange for a chance at a new life.

Madho Singh and peace team members went - at considerable risk - to talk to the heads of the many dacoit gangs in the area. J.P. Narayan went to speak with public officials. A peace village was built were the bandits could voluntarily surrender, learn new skills, secure financial support for starting a different way of life, and repair some of the harms they had done. The bandits would be held accountable for their crimes, but they would not be hung - the common punishment in those days. In exchange, the bandits gained a number of other important promises: their family members would be kept safe from reprisals by members of rival gangs, the enemies of high profile dacoits who participated in the program would be disarmed to stop the cycle of reprisals, and the peace workers would ensure that the police stopped harassing the dacoits' families. The bandits agreed to immediately release all kidnapped persons, cease collecting punitive taxes, and refrain from further banditry-related activities.

Peace workers also held healing processes for police, bandits, and families, including what we might call restorative justice processes. They organized legal aid to defend the charges against dacoits. Educational programs were provided. There were no uniforms, no locks on the doors, and the bandits were free to leave at any time - though they would forfeit the benefits of the program if they returned to the gangs.

As unbelievable as this sounds, it worked. The peace village held several formal surrender ceremonies. Over a number of years, 450 dacoits turned themselves in.

Discussion Questions:

- Is there ever a time when someone is undeserving of a "second chance"?
- What are the benefits of giving people a second chance? What are the challenges?

- An End To Bandits -

What is causing so many people to become bandits?

Alaren was pleased with Second Chance Village, as the bandits' village came to be called, but he wasn't entirely satisfied. New people arrived each week, sent by the Hooded Hunter. According to their tales, they'd broken laws back home - killed a man, stolen some gold - and feared the gallows and the death penalty. The soldiers maintained the unofficial amnesty Alaren had arranged, so long as the former bandits obeyed the laws of the village.

But it was a tenuous solution at best. Even the Hooded Hunter refused to give up his banditry, telling Alaren that he couldn't trust the soldiers not to string him up or ship him downriver to be hanged.

Alaren thought the whole situation was ridiculous. The same former bandits who were so peacefully tilling the fields and shearing sheep in Second Chance Village could also be doing those same things back in their original homes. The laws of his brother, King Marin, were driving people into banditry because they feared the hangman's noose. If Marin really wanted to end banditry, Alaren thought, he'd work out some other form of justice.

Finally, Alaren realized he'd have to sail downriver and try to persuade his brother. He still had a promise to keep to the

Hooded Hunter; the book of bandit tales had to be shared far and wide.

On the night before he departed, he was camped by the river waiting for the south barge when the Hooded Hunter came to find him.

"I have a favor to ask," the bandit told Alaren. "On the west bank of the Mari River, across from Marin's house, there is a home with a lion's head carved on the door. Please tell the occupants that I am well - only that and nothing else or I'll track you down and slice out your tongue."

Alaren agreed. He departed at dawn and made his way downriver to the city. There, he found the house with the lion on the door and knocked. He learned that the son of the house had vanished years ago after killing a lord in a duel. Guessing that the Hooded Hunter was that son, Alaren said only that the man was alive and well, and that he couldn't say any more than that.

Next, he brought the bandit tales to the National Library and persuaded the scribes to make several copies for him. One he took to a typesetter to be published and circulated. The other, he brought with him when he went to pay his respects to Marin.

"Brother," Alaren said to Marin, "I have an idea for how you could stop bandits, crime, and violence all at once."

"Hang them all from the nearest gallows?" Marin answered testily, raising an eyebrow at his youngest brother.

"You've tried that and it's not working," Alaren pointed out. "I think, instead of hanging them, you should hire them."

Marin threw an alarmed look at Alaren. His stork-like troublemaker of a brother simply smiled and explained. He wanted Marin to form a peace force out of the people who were most likely to cause violence and crime. Their job would be to stop the violence and intervene in crimes. Instead of hanging people as thieves or forcing them to run to the hills to become bandits, Alaren thought Marin could hire them to solve his problem at its roots.

"How do you know this will work?" Marin asked him skeptically.

"I don't," Alaren answered honestly. "But we know hanging them doesn't stop more people from taking their place. At least give this a try."

So, Marin reluctantly agreed to the experiment. He suspended the death laws for a year and made his judges send the criminals to Alaren's new Peace Force chapter. The people received training then were sent out into the city in teams. They broke up fights. They stopped feuds. They found thieves and secured employment for them instead. By the end of the year, the Hooded Hunter sent Alaren a message: *Keep it up. It's working.*

Not a single new bandit had appeared in the hills.

"Give me another year, Marin," Alaren requested, "and I'll wager we will have cut violence and crime in half, at least."

Marin agreed. The record of their conversation is lost to the crumbling annals of time, but we do know that Alaren, armed with truth, also convinced Marin to overturn the death laws once and for all, and offer pardon to any bandit who would make restitution for harm done.

By midsummer the following year, the last of the foothill bandits ceased to plague the region. In the house with a lion's head carved on the door, the Hooded Hunter returned home, no longer hiding his identity with a mask or a hood. He married his childhood sweetheart and had a son who grew up reading Alaren's bandit tales, never suspecting that the notorious Hooded Hunter was actually his father.

Alaren had learned an important lesson: peace and justice were tied together tighter than the tightest knot. To ensure peace, he had to stop the bandits. To stop the bandits, he had to give them a second chance. To give them a second chance, he had to change the laws. To change the laws, he had to tell true stories. To tell true stories, he had to listen. And to listen, he had to make peace with the very same bandits who had once wanted to kill him.

Peace isn't made by kings. It is made by the person who offers it first, despite the odds and in spite of the dangers. Any of us can be that person.

~ The End ~

Behind the Story - Real Life Inspiration
Operation Peacemaker

"When they outlaw life, only outlaws live." Beneath problems of crime are often economic injustices that make it impossible for people to pay their bills and put food on the table. If we want to stop crime, the answer isn't more and harsher punishments; it's more fair and sane policies.

Ending violence is also connected to trauma healing, social-emotional skills, conflict resolution skills, and a network of other issues. Prison sentences, harsh punishments, and the death penalty don't necessarily reduce crime and violence. In some cases, they aggravate the problem.

In 2009, Richmond, CA, was ranked the most violent city in the United States. Its homicide rate was three times higher than Chicago. Public officials suspected that 17 gang members were responsible for 70% of the violence. In 2010, an unusual - and often controversial - new program called Operation Peacemaker was launched. The designer and director, DeVone Boggan, asked each public official to send him the seventeen names independently of the others. This yielded 28 individuals. Of these, three died of gun-related violence before the program launched. The remaining 25 were invited to a meeting on the issue of gang-related violence; 21 showed up.

Boggan began by apologizing. He said the City of Richmond should have invited these important people to be a part of the solution earlier. He ended the meeting by giving them all $1,000 cash. News about Operation Peacemaker exploded across social media.

But money alone doesn't stop violence. Boggan's program engaged the 21 men in a weekly training program that taught them how to intervene and de-escalate violence. Operation Peacemaker organized and deployed teams that could deal with the conflicts. The program also offered support for the participants, connecting them to job training, mentorship, and social services. After six months in the program, the participants could receive up to $1000/month. The exact amount varied by individual and was based on making steady progress toward their goals, such as paying off parking tickets, getting addiction treatment, getting a drivers license, or finding safe housing.

Operation Peacemaker had two other important aspects: mentorship by African-American elders (an important group for these younger men) and a firewall between the program and the police. Operation Peacemaker was not run by the police department and no information was shared with the police. This was critical for many of the participating gang members.

Did it work? Yes.

Over seven years, they reduced gun violence by an average of 50%. By 2017, the four Peacemaker cohorts involved 84 people. The program had a dropout rate of zero. On top of that, 79 out of the 84 Peacemakers (selected because they were highly likely to either commit or become victims of gun violence) are still alive.

Operation Peacemaker shows that if we want to get to the roots of crime and violence, we have to do a lot more than lock people up (or hang them in the case of Alaren's story). By engaging the most-impacted in being part of the solution, we can find practical and effective ways to not only stop the problem, but heal the underlying causes.

Discussion Questions:

- What does one need to do to earn a "second chance"?
- Is it possible to change the culture of an entire community?
- Why might people who are likely to cause violence be the best at stopping violence?
- Do you think Operation Peacemaker would have worked if it had *only* paid people? How did the other components of the program contribute to its success?

- Steal This Story -
You can't steal what's freely given.

Alaren stared into the flames of a fire as the light danced across the mounded snow. He pulled his cloak tighter as his soup boiled. Once again, he had stopped on a lonely trailside in the early nightfall to rest his feet and fill his stomach before the next stretch of the journey through darkness. He knew these paths across the Border Mountains like the lines in his face . . . more and more of which were appearing each year.

A footstep behind him broke his thoughts. He turned. A man with a drawn sword and desperate eyes stood tensely on the edge of the firelight.

"Give me your purse or I'll kill you," the man threatened.

"There is nothing in my purse except for a handful of flour to make flatbread," Alaren answered calmly. "Sit down and eat my soup with me. I'll make bread for you in the bottom of the pot."

He gestured to the log next to him.

The robber stared at him in confusion.

"I'm robbing you," he stated.

"No, you're not," Alaren retorted. "You can't steal from me what I give freely to you. Sit down and put that sword away. It's too cold for sword fighting tonight."

The man hesitated. Alaren slowly stirred the soup. The

steam carried the savory aroma toward the robber. He lowered the sword, sighed, and sat down next to Alaren.

"Thank you," the man said in a gruff, slightly embarrassed voice.

"No, thank you," Alaren answered. "You've relieved my loneliness on this dark night. Tell me something - a joke, a story, your life's tale - anything to drive off the distances aching in my bones."

He poured some soup into his tin cup and handed it to the man. As he sipped from the pot with his traveling spoon, Alaren listened as the man began to tell stories: old folktales, newly-spun myths, bawdy jokes, ridiculous but true stories from up and down the mountains. Alaren laughed until his sides ached at the humorous stories and brushed away tears at the sad tales. As he moistened flour and began to fry bread in the bottom of the now-empty soup pot, he asked the man how he came to his latest profession.

"As a robber?" the man stammered, turning red. "Hunger recruited me. I was a farmer, but my farm burned in the war. I have nothing now."

Alaren flipped the bread.

"You have stories . . . . that is something."

"A man can't live on legends alone," the fellow replied bitterly.

Alaren pulled the bread out of the pot and tossed it from hand to hand to cool it. He tore it in half and gave it to the man.

"Consider this proposal as we break bread," Alaren suggested. "Travel with me. Eat at my hearth. Work at my side. I have only one request."

The man shifted nervously, wondering what outrageous claim the odd stranger was about to demand.

"Tell my stories," Alaren whispered, a light shining in his eyes. "Tell the tales of the Way Between and the work we are doing for peace. Remember them and share them on your journeys. Teach them to the children and to the grandparents of each village we visit. A storyteller as good as you will be welcome and fed in any village!"

The man laughed and agreed. How could he not? Telling stories was the best job in the whole world!

It is because of this man - whose name has been lost to time, even as his story has endured over centuries - that we know of Alaren today. The bulk of Alaren's adventures are known because the Way Between guided Alaren to invite a hungry man to share his meal instead of attacking the would-be robber and driving him away.

May we all follow in Alaren's footsteps, embody the Way Between, share its stories, and work for peace in our world.

~ The End ~

Behind the Story - Real Life Inspiration
The Robber and The Glass of Wine

This Alaren tale is inspired by a story about a dinner party in a suburban city in the United States that was interrupted by an armed robber. After several of the men tried to intimidate the robber into leaving, a woman did something surprising: she offered him a glass of wine. That de-escalated the tension and opened up other possibilities for changing the situation. In the end, the robber left without stealing anything or hurting anyone. You can watch a wonderful animated version of this story by Invisibilia on Youtube.

There are stories about Mohandas K. Gandhi that share similar elements. Once, a man tried to rob him and Gandhi gave the robber everything he had, sparing the man from the negative karma of being a thief. Another time, Gandhi was boarding a departing train when his sandal fell off. Without blinking, he pulled the other sandal from his foot and tossed it behind him onto the platform. "That way," he said, "whoever finds them will have a matching pair."

In a way, sharing *The Adventures of Alaren* with friends and family is like tossing our shoes onto the platform for someone else to wear. These are the stories that we all need to step into in order to walk the path of peace. It's helpful to have a matching set. Thank you for sharing these stories far and wide with everyone you know.

Discussion Questions:

- Who could you share these stories with?
- Have you ever done an unexpected act of kindness, such as Alaren did with the would-be robber? What happened?

- Beyond Life -

Alaren died as an old man - a miracle for a person who leapt between violence and war his whole life. His children had children when he finally breathed his last breath. He died in his bed in the Way Station he had built in the Middle Pass. But the folktales say he never truly died. In spirit, he wandered the land for centuries, making peace, stopping wars, and ending fights. Ghost stories, legends, and myths about Alaren took on a life of their own.

- Alaren's Death & Funeral -

His spirit still strives for peace.

When the passing years and turning seasons whitened Alaren's hair and deepened the furrows of his wrinkles, he stayed close to the hearth at his Way Station in the Middle Pass. Instead of trekking over mountain and valley, hill and dale, he stayed home and people came to visit him. His Peace Force set up a school close by and trained the next generation to continue the work of peace.

The time for Alaren's next great adventure arrived. One morning, when he went to rise at first light, his spirit slipped from his body and stood staring down at the bed in surprise. He felt wonderful - the aches in his bones had disappeared; the tiredness in his limbs had vanished - but when his daughter and granddaughter found him dead, his heart grew sad for their sorrow.

His spirit lingered around the Way Station as his family and friends gathered. They prepared his body for burial. They sent messenger hawks east, west, north, and south to tell everyone the news. They announced the date of the memorial ceremony.

The hawks flew out and returned with kind condolences and an astonishing promise: people were making peace in honor of Alaren. Bandits and soldiers settled old grievances. Feuding clans ended decades-long grudges. Quarrelling family members forgave each other. The sons of Marin and Shirar signed a ceasefire agreement, stopping their latest set of skirmishes.

I should have died years ago, Alaren's spirit thought with a chuckle and a sigh.

On the day of his memorial, tens of thousands of people gathered. His nephews and nieces came from Shirar's city and Marin's river island. Desert dwellers, river valley people, Border Mountain villagers all came by the thousands. Though skirmishes had heated up in the past years, all weapons were set aside. For the two weeks of gatherings, not a single act of violence occurred, anywhere. People told stories, one after another, of all the ways Alaren and his Peace Force had helped them. Bards sang ballads of his adventures. People honored him by training in the Way Between.

Alaren's spirit watched it all with a bemused smile . . . why did he have to die for people to finally take his life work so seriously?

At last, the end of the ceremony came. One by one, people departed for their homes. The day came when Alaren saw the spirits of his long-departed wife and so many of the people he once knew. They beckoned to him from the place beyond. Alaren strode toward them into a light that gleamed brighter than the sun. A sense of peace so profound it brought tears to his eyes flooded through him. He clasped his wife's hand. They turned to walk to the next realm.

Then Alaren stopped.

From the world of the living, a harsh clang struck. He heard shouts. The sounds of fighting broke out.

"My love," he murmured to his wife's spirit.

She kissed him.

"I know," she answered, "go."

253

Then Alaren turned back and returned to the world as a spirit, wandering the hills and valleys to wage peace for ever more.

~ The End ~

Behind the Story - Real Life Inspiration
Badshah Khan's Funeral

The story of a ceasefire in honor of Alaren comes from the true story of Badshah Khan's passing. This man, a contemporary of Gandhi's, had formed the world's largest "Peace Army", an 80,000-100,000 person nonviolent group called the "Servants of God". When Abdul Ghaffar Khan (called "Badshah" in respect) died under house arrest in Pakistan, thousands of people marched in the funeral procession that carried his body to Afghanistan, his homeland. During the march through the Khyber Pass, after two bombings killed fifteen people, both sides of the Soviet-Afghan War declared a ceasefire to allow the funeral procession to pass.

In this fictional story, Alaren's spirit pauses at the threshold of the realm beyond death. Hearing the sounds of fighting in the world, he turns back to continue to help people stop war. This part of the story is drawn from the Buddhist bodhisattvas who turn back from *nirvana* upon hearing the cries of suffering in the world. Devoting themselves to ending suffering, they postpone enlightenment until all beings can also reach that state of understanding.

Alaren continues his work for peace as a spirit, just as all the people who have come before us continue to inspire us to work for peace and justice. In our own lives, as we draw upon the stories and examples of people like Gandhi, King, and so many more, we keep their spirits alive in our hearts and honor their courageous lives with our own.

Discussion Questions:

- Who inspires you to work for peace and justice?
- Do you have a favorite inspiring story about peace and nonviolence? If so, where did you first hear it?
- What are some places where we can find and share stories like Alaren's or the real life inspirations included in this book with other people?

Acknowledgements

A book like this comes into the world with the support of so many people. I have been reading and collecting stories of nonviolence in action for years. Older peace activists have sent me books from their personal libraries. In particular, my friend, colleague, and teacher Tom Hastings sent me a very illuminating, out-of-print 2002 Peace Calendar that shared 52 Stories of Nonviolent Success. The Global Nonviolent Action Database has also been a vital resource, as has my work with Nonviolence Now, Metta Center for Nonviolence, and Campaign Nonviolence.

A special thank-you goes out to three people who read the manuscript and offered invaluable feedback. Robin Wildman, founder of the Nonviolent Schools Project and retired 5th grade teacher helped coral my wild imagination into a format that young people would enjoy as much as older readers. She also offered many of the discussion questions in this book, and revised my initial attempts. Thank you!

Michael Colvin, peace activist and writer, also read the manuscript of this book and pointed out typos (any remaining are entirely my fault), inconsistencies, and very helpful suggestions on how to improve the stories. My friend Nina Koevoets, an international nonviolence trainer and co-author of *Engaging Nonviolence* as well as a children's book on protecting the earth, graciously lent me her perspective and support in crafting discussion questions. My deepest gratitude goes out to you all!

Leslie Donovan, a professor at University of New Mexico Honors College, connected me to the idea of creating a different mythology. Her interest in Tolkien's writings and the Mythopoeic Society lit the spark of curiosity that helped me write these stories.

These stories truly wouldn't have been possible without the real-life people who inspired them. Many are not known to me personally, but I would like to acknowledge those who are: David Hartsough, Kathy Kelly, Kevin Zeese and Margaret Flowers, Michael Nagler, Stephanie Van Hook, Kit Miller, Heart Phoenix, Jeffrey Weisberg, Medea Benjamin, Jodie Evans, the Afghan Peace Volunteers, Sherri Maurin, Tom Hastings, Paul DeMain (and many others in Wisconsin), Dena Eakles and Echo Valley Hope, Sherri Mitchell, David Swanson and World Beyond War, Veronica Pelicaric and Campaign Nonviolence, and so many more.

I wish to thank all the readers of the Ari Ara Series. Your enthusiasm and kind words fueled this project. It is always inspiring to write for a ready audience. The early readers of the online version of this book, *Stories of the Third Brother*, have been wonderfully supportive and patient. Their faith and enthusiasm kept me going through the headaches of the revision process. To all of the fans of Ari Ara's series, I am delighted to finally bring this collection of Alaren stories to you in paperback and ebook versions.

Last, but certainly not least, my partner Dariel Garner is indispensable to the writing process. Thank you.

Rivera Sun

ABOUT THE AUTHOR

Rivera Sun is the author of *The Way Between, The Lost Heir, The Dandelion Insurrection* and other novels, as well as theatrical plays, a study guide to nonviolent action, three volumes of poetry, and numerous articles. She has red hair, a twin sister, and a fondness for esoteric mystics. She went to Bennington College to study writing as a Harcourt Scholar and graduated with a degree in dance. She lives in an earthship house in New Mexico, where she writes essays and novels. She is a trainer in strategy for nonviolent movements and an activist. Rivera has been an aerial dancer, a bike messenger, and a gung-fu style tea server. Everything else about her - except her writing - is perfectly ordinary.

Rivera Sun also loves hearing from her readers:
Email: info@riverasun.com
Facebook: Rivera Sun
Twitter: @RiveraSunAuthor
Website: www.riverasun.com

Read all of the adventures in the Ari Ara Series!
The Way Between, The Lost Heir, and Desert Song

The Way Between

Between flight and fight lies a mysterious third path called *The Way Between*, and young shepherdess and orphan Ari Ara must master it . . . before war destroys everything she loves! She begins training as the apprentice of the great warrior Shulen, and enters a world of warriors and secrets, swords and magic, friendship and mystery.

The Lost Heir

Going beyond dragon-slayers and sword-swingers, *The Lost Heir* blends fantasy and adventure with social justice issues in an unstoppable story that will make you cheer! Mariana Capital is in an uproar. The splendor of the city dazzles Ari Ara until she makes a shocking discovery . . . the luxury of the nobles is built by the forced labor of the desert people.

Desert Song

Exiled to the desert, Ari Ara is thrust between the warriors trying to grab power . . . and the women rising up to stop them! Every step she takes propels her deeper into trouble: her trickster horse bolts, her friend is left for dead, and Ari Ara has to run away to save him. But time is running out - can she find him before it's too late?

**If you enjoyed *The Adventures of Alaren*,
you'll love the Ari Ara Series!**

**Enjoy this excerpt from *The Way Between*
Book One of the Ari Ara Series**

The Horns of Monk's Hand bellowed low and sonorous. Ari Ara skidded to a halt. As the deep tones rolled around the echoing bowl of the valley, the girl's blue-grey eyes traced the sound back to the stone-carved monastery far below. The Horns announced the change of seasons. Autumn had arrived.

She leapt across the black rocks of the High Mountains. The wind flung back the hood of her thick, black wool shepherdess cloak. Her red hair burned bright against the steep slopes. The sky blazed cold blue. The wind nearly knocked her off her feet.

As she hurtled down the outcropping, she put her fingers in her mouth and whistled. Sharp and distinctive, the tone shrilled high then low. It was a Fanten call, one that echoed through the forests below on dark nights before moonrise. In the meadow, the tall black-fleeced Fanten sheep lifted their heads.

Autumn! Ari Ara leapt off the ledge and landed in a crouch. She shivered, glancing up at the ferocious blue sky. Cold gripped the air on the higher ridges. The silver mists hinted of snow. Ari Ara jogged toward the high altitude meadow where her flock grazed. She had the build of a shepherdess - wiry and strong, muscles tight to bones, eyes that scanned the distances, and a sense of the wide sky in her stance. Her cheeks reddened with the cold, skin already roughened by the harsh winds of the High Mountains. A pair of worn, ragged boots bound her legs up to her knees. Her breeches vanished beneath a tunic. On top, she wore a shepherdess cloak felted tight enough to keep out the rain and snow.

Again, the Horns sounded, calling the farmers in from the harvest. Ari Ara raced around a tumble of rocks into the golden grasses and skidded to a stop among the sheep. The lead ewe flicked her ears at the girl and trotted over. Ari Ara stretched out her hand in greeting. The warm breath of the sheep's muzzle tickled her palm. The wind chilled it quickly. Like all Fanten sheep, the long-legged ewe stood nearly four feet tall at her back. She was old; her fleece had silvered nearly to white. The days of her coal-black youth had long passed, but the strands of her fleece still stretched the length of Ari Ara's arm. Fanten sheep were considered the finest in all of Mariana, but they would only live in the High Mountains, not in the lowlands down by Mari River and the Capital. Rumors claimed that the uncanny black sheep followed only Fanten shepherdesses, but Ari Ara knew it was familiarity and trust - not the scent of the Fanten in her blood - that brought the sheep to her.

She was an orphan. No one knew her parentage and no one cared. No one - Fanten, monk, or villager - claimed her as one of their kind. *Ari Ara*, she was named, *not this, not that.* A child who belonged to no one, but roamed the wide bowl of the crater valley, the deep forests, and the High Mountains on her own. Shaped like the fingers of a meditating monk, the Monk's Hand Mountains loomed dark, mysterious, and serene. The villagers' fields and houses nestled in the broad, flat palm. The Thumb's Pass met the Forefinger Ridge in a narrow opening where the river rushed down into Mari Valley. The Fanten Forest covered the sharp, forbidding slopes of the three Fingers - a series of deep ravines carved by rivers, wind, and time. This rugged landscape formed the outer range of her world. It took a full day to cross the crater valley and years to explore the looming mountains. Ari Ara knew the High Mountains well from her time watching the Fanten flock. Monk's Hand had grown as familiar as her own.

"Autumn has arrived," Ari Ara told the ewe, nodding to the peaks as the Horns of Monk's Hand Monastery thundered again. "It's time to go down the mountain."

The mother bleated. The flock echoed the call. Ari Ara spun and took off at a run. She did not look back. Once the lead ewe understood, the flock would always follow. The girl leapt over the boulders and the sheep flowed behind her.

At the crossroads, they turned onto the narrow path to the right, snaking down toward the shelter of the Fanten Forest. Massive trees towered overhead, anchored with a web of connected roots that ran vast distances beneath the earth. Under the boughs, the air hung cool and still. The thud of the sheep's hooves fell muffled as they trotted along the thick carpet of needles. With their black, shining wool, the sheep slid through the dark shadowed wood, nearly invisible.

The silver-haired Fanten Grandmother, headwoman of the group, stood waiting in the inner grove. Ari Ara halted, chest heaving and cheeks burning with warmth. You could never sneak up on a Fanten . . . though they startled everyone else with their secretive ways, silent footsteps, and sudden appearances. In the carved caves under the bases of the trees, the Fanten lived warm and protected.

"Well, now," the old woman spoke in her own tongue, greeting the mother ewe. "How did she care for you this summer?"

The little woman stood just barely taller than Ari Ara. Her silver-white Fanten cloak came from the mother ewe's back. The ewe laid her muzzle in the cupped hands of the grandmother. They studied each other in a long and silent exchange.

Ari Ara waited for the verdict, thinking back over the season. She remembered how a late snowstorm caught them in the upper meadows, how she brought the flock to shelter, how she struggled all night to help a pair of tangled twin lambs into the world, how a wolf pack snatched one of them away and would have taken more if Ari Ara had not raced like a howling red-haired demon into their midst, hurling stones and sticks.

"Good," spoke the Fanten Grandmother. She released the mother's muzzle and stretched her wrinkled hand toward the girl.

"You've grown," she commented, her dark eyes scanning the girl. "You're tall compared to the Fanten daughters, though still short by Marianan standards. You've been like that since the beginning."

Ari Ara looked up, hopeful. Perhaps the elder would share more of her past - something more than: *you were left here as an infant. We cared for you until you were old enough to watch the sheep. Then we sent you into the mountains with the flock.*

The sheep choose the shepherd, and to the Fanten's surprise, the mother ewe picked the flame-haired Ari Ara. The village boys teased her about having a sheep for a mother - but only when she descended from the High Mountains. Otherwise, they steered clear of the Fanten sheep and the wild shepherdess. The villagers' white sheep liked thicker fields. The black Fanten flocks preferred silence, solitude, and space.

"What will you do this winter, child?" the elder asked.

"I could stay here and learn the sacred dances," Ari Ara suggested hopefully.

The intricate dances of the Fanten fascinated her. She'd grown up watching the women, even learning the common ones that all the young Fanten daughters knew. But last year, Fanten Grandmother had put a stop to that, saying that Ari Ara was not one of them and had to seek her own path.

Today, the Fanten Grandmother's eyes clouded and her mouth turned down at the corners.

"It is not your fate to follow the Fanten path."

Ari Ara scowled and cursed fate. Who gave that the final say? Not her. She kicked sullenly at the ground.

"Maybe I'll just go back into the mountains and live in a cave," she grumbled.

"Don't be ridiculous," the Fanten Grandmother snapped. "Go to the village like you did last year."

"I can't," she muttered, scuffing the needles on the ground with her heel. "The village leader threw me out midwinter for causing trouble."

"And did you?" the wrinkled old woman demanded.

"Not half as much as I wanted to," Ari Ara admitted fiercely.

The elder hid a smile.

"You ought to learn to read and write," she told her.

Ari Ara made a face.

"What good is book learning to a shepherdess?" she complained.

"You won't be a shepherdess forever."

The Fanten Grandmother's voice rang prophetically, snapping Ari Ara out of her sulking. She stared at the old woman who stood silver and white against the black shadows of the trees. The elder's dark eyes gazed at the swaying boughs. The wind whispered secrets in the glossy needles. She tilted her head as if listening. Ari Ara's blue-grey eyes lifted, but she saw only the outlines of branches against the sky beyond. She sensed, as she always did, that the mysterious Fanten knew far more than they revealed.

The Fanten Grandmother dropped her gaze to the girl. She sighed. That child was always pushing fate . . . and it would get her into trouble one day.

"Go to the village and apologize to the leader," she told the girl firmly.

Ari Ara sighed and didn't reply.

Swiftly, before the girl asked any more questions, the old Fanten bent, kissed the crown of the girl's bright red hair and said the ritual words, "Thank you for keeping our flock safe. We honor you for that gift."

Ari Ara accepted the ritual words moodily.

The delicate old woman pursed her lips and sounded her whistle. She turned into the forest; the mother ewe and flock followed. Ari Ara stared after her for a moment, then spun on her heel and ran off in the other direction. Hearing her soft footsteps departing, the Fanten Grandmother paused. Her eyes widened, remembering.

"Ari Ara!" she called.

But it was too late. The flame of her hair vanished.

The child was gone.

**Find *The Way Between* and all of the Ari Ara Series
on any major online bookstore or on Rivera Sun's website:
www.riverasun.com**

Praise for Rivera Sun's
The Dandelion Insurrection

A rare gem of a book, a must read, it charts the way forward in this time of turmoil and transformation." - Velcrow Ripper, director Occupy Love, Genie Award Winner

 "When fear is used to control us, love is how we rebel!" Under a gathering storm of tyranny, Zadie Byrd Gray whirls into the life of Charlie Rider and asks him to become the voice of the Dandelion Insurrection. With the rallying cry of life, liberty, and love, Zadie and Charlie fly across America leaving a wake of revolution in their path. Passion erupts. Danger abounds. The lives of millions hang by a thin thread of courage, but in the midst of the madness, the golden soul of humanity blossoms . . . and miracles start to unfold!

"This novel will not only make you want to change the world, it will remind you that you can." - Gayle Brandeis, author of *The Book of Dead Birds*, winner of the Bellwether Prize for Socially Engaged Fiction

"Close your eyes and imagine the force of the people and the power of love overcoming the force of greed and the love of power. Then read *The Dandelion Insurrection*. In a world where despair has deep roots, *The Dandelion Insurrection* bursts forth with joyful abandon." - Medea Benjamin, Co-founder of CodePink

"THE handbook for the coming revolution!" - Lo Daniels, Editor of Dandelion Salad

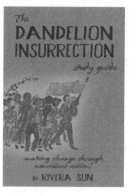

Praise for *The Roots of Resistance*

You're in for an exciting ride as incendiary writer Charlie Rider and the unforgettable Zadie Byrd Gray rise to meet the political challenges flung at them from all sides. Freedom and equality loom just out of reach as the outraged corporate oligarchy scrambles to take back power after the Dandelion Insurrection's successful nonviolent revolution. Everyone from schoolteachers to whistleblowers leaps into action to help them confront the forces of corrupt politics. But the struggle turns volatile when an armed group called the Roots shows up. They claim to be protecting the movement . . . but who do they really serve?

"If you loved Starhawk's *Fifth Sacred Thing*, if you loved recently-departed Ursula K. LeGuin's *The Dispossessed*, if you admire the spirit of the Standing Rock Water Protectors, you will drink in this must-read page-turner . . . an epic story that will move your spirit, bringing tears to your eyes and healing to your soul." – Rosa Zubizarreta, Author of *From Conflict to Creative Collaboration*

"Rivera Sun always gifts us with usefully creative fiction. Her *Roots of Resistance* – the second novel of her Dandelion Trilogy – offers an inspiring story to help guide love-based strategic change efforts . . . . It takes a storyteller like Rivera Sun who inspires us to rise to the challenge as her characters do, because her stories tell us how."
– Tom Atlee, Co-Intelligence Institute.

Reader Praise for Rivera Sun's
Steam Drills, Treadmills, and Shooting Stars

Steam Drills, Treadmills, and Shooting Stars is a story about people just like you, filled with the audacity of hope and fueled by the passion of unstoppable love. The ghost of folk hero John Henry haunts Jack Dalton, a corporate lawyer for Standard Coal as Henrietta Owens, activist and mother, wakes up the nation with some tough-loving truth about the environment, the economy, justice, and hope. Pressures mount as John Henry challenges Jack to stand up to the steam drills of contemporary America . . . before it's too late.

'This book is a gem and I'm going to put it in my jewelry box!"

"It 'dips your head in a bucket of truth'."

"This is not a page turner . . . it stops you in your tracks and makes you revel in the beauty of the written word."

"Epic, mythic . . .it's like going to church and praying for the salvation of yourself and your people and your country."

"Controversial, political, and so full of love."

"Partway through reading, I realized I was participating in a historical event. This book has changed me and will change everyone who reads it."

"I am sixty-two years old, and I cried for myself, my neighbors, our country and the earth. I cried and am so much better for it. I would recommend this book to everyone."

Praise for Rivera Sun's *Billionaire Buddha*

From fabulous wealth to unlimited blessings, the price of enlightenment may bankrupt billionaire Dave Grant. Emotionally destitute in the prime of his career, he searches for love and collides with Joan Hathaway. The encounter rattles his soul and unravels his world. Capitalism, property, wealth, mansions: his notions of success crumble into dust. From toasting champagne on top of the world to swigging whiskey with bums in the gutter, Dave Grant's journey is an unforgettable ride that leaves you cheering!

". . . inspirational and transformational! An enjoyable read for one's heart and soul."
-Chuck Collins, senior scholar, Institute for Policy Studies; co-author with Bill Gates Sr. of 'Wealth and Our Commonwealth'

". . . inspiring a skeptic is no easy task and Rivera Sun manages to do so, gracefully, convincingly, and admirably."
- Casey Dorman, Editor-in-Chief, Lost Coast Review

"People, if you haven't gotten your copy of *Billionaire Buddha* yet, you are letting a rare opportunity slip through your fingers. It's that good."
- Burt Kempner, screenwriter, producer and author of children's books

"This is the kind of book that hits you in the gut and makes you stop and think about what you just read."
- Rob Garvey, reader

"A clear and conscious look at our times and the dire need for a real change to heart based living."
- Carol Ranellone, reader

Made in the USA
Middletown, DE
01 November 2021